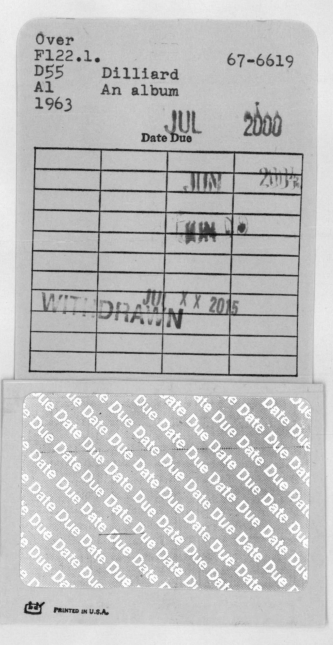

An Album of
New Netherland

New Amsterdam, now New York on Manhattan Island.

This is known as the Prototype View because many later drawings have been based on it. It is a water color 24 1/2 by 16 1/4 inches. Made after the surrender, it shows the city between the autumn of 1650 and the summer of 1653. At the left, Fort Amsterdam and the windmill tower above the houses on t' Water (the Strand). At the extreme right is the Stadt Huys. The original belongs to the Dutch government, which lent it to the Museum of the City of New York in the 1940's.

AN ALBUM OF
New Netherland

BY MAUD ESTHER DILLIARD

WITH A FOREWORD
BY V. ISABELLE MILLER
CURATOR OF
COSTUMES, FURNITURE
AND SILVER
AT THE
MUSEUM OF THE
CITY OF NEW YORK

BRAMHALL HOUSE: NEW YORK

67-6619

Library of Congress Catalog Card No. 63-9904

THIS BOOK IS DEDICATED

TO MY SISTER

Marion Kenny (Dilliard) Halpine

ACKNOWLEDGMENTS

A NUMBER *of years ago, I was asked by the Holland House Corporation of The Netherlands, then with headquarters at 10 Rockefeller Plaza in New York, to assemble an exhibition of articles which had belonged to the colonists of New Netherland. It was a unique collection that I was able to gather together, for many of the antiques were family treasures which had seldom, if ever, been displayed publicly. Billed as an Exhibition of Dutch Colonial Heirlooms, their showing drew more than 7,000 visitors in the ten weeks of its existence.*

The great interest taken in the heirlooms led me to compile the present work. A few of the photographs in it were made for the Holland House Corporation's scrapbook by Boutrelle of New York. The others were obtained especially for this book. This was made possible through the kindness of many people. The curators of museums, the directors of historical societies, the domines of Dutch Reformed churches, and my many friends among the descendants of New Netherlanders have been most generous in granting me access to the treasures which they possess, and to each and every one of them I wish to express my deep appreciation.

Special thanks are due Miss V. Isabelle Miller of the Museum of the City of New York; Miss Janet McFarlane and Mr. Norman Rice of the Albany Institute of History and Art; Mr. Marvin Schwartz of the Brooklyn Museum; Mr. Loring McMillan and Miss Margery Kerr of the Staten Island Historical

8

Society; Mr. Robert G. Wheeler of Sunnyside Restoration; Miss Betty Ezequelle of the New-York Historical Society; the librarian of the Netherlands Information Service of New York; and the staff of the Long Island Historical Society, who were most helpful in enabling me to procure photographs and answers to my many inquiries. I deeply appreciate all they have done for me. Acknowledgments for the photographs appear at the ends of the captions.

The translation of Sarah Rapalje's wedding medal was made for me by Professor Adriaan J. Barnow of Columbia University. To Mr. Clay Lancaster I owe a debt of gratitude for his many helpful suggestions while I was preparing this manuscript and for the time he spent reading it.

MAUD ESTHER DILLIARD
BROOKLYN HEIGHTS,
NEW YORK

Table of Contents

Foreword

EARLY *in the 17th century a group of hardy pioneers settled Manhattan Island, nearby coasts, and established themselves as far up the river which Henry Hudson had discovered as the present Albany. The majority of these settlers were from The Netherlands, and their flourishing colony on the tip of Manhattan Island was destined to become the nucleus of Dutch culture and influence in the New World for almost two hundred years.*

The strong influence of Holland may be attributed to the solid character of the Dutch burghers who immigrated and their deep love for the mother country, which was passed on through each generation. The laws of the new homeland were respected, and in this orderly atmosphere the arts and crafts, which had reached a high level of excellence in Holland of the 16th century, were transplanted to the New World. Craftsmen who had brought their skills with them became the native cabinetmakers, silversmiths, and such who taught the youth by the same exacting standards they had learned to follow. These indigenous artisans, in turn, produced beautiful examples of European forms adapted to the local tastes.

This book is a welcome addition to those few which have already appeared to call our attention to the first fifty years' history and culture of this famous island. The illustrations tell the story of how our ancestors lived and with what comforts they were surrounded. These objects pictured have been selected with loving care and with an eye to their history to ascertain that they were actually in use here in the 17th century. It will be readily seen in this handsome book that the rich culture of Holland was appreciated and passed on to succeeding generations.

It has often been said that the position occupied by the wife and mother throws light on the civilization of any society. It is a well-authenticated fact that the women of New Netherland of the 17th century were more highly educated, better protected by the laws of the country, and held a more prominent position than any of their contemporaries in other countries. The girls received the same education as the boys and shared in their studies until the latter were old enough to select a trade or profession for themselves. The girls were then carefully trained in household duties and educated to fill responsible positions.

For anyone interested at all in the culture and life of our ancestors, this book will add enlightenment and foster enthusiasm for the further study of these arts and crafts.

The photographs have been selected from major collections of Dutch material in this area and from private sources. It is a wonderful fount of information for those of Dutch ancestry and those interested in the general history of Manhattan. What an excellent book to interest people in the early history of our land!

V. ISABELLE MILLER
CURATOR OF COSTUMES, FURNITURE, AND SILVER
MUSEUM OF THE CITY OF NEW YORK

General Introduction

NEW NETHERLAND was that portion of the North American Continent which in the 17th century the States General of The United Provinces of the Netherlands claimed for the Dutch nation. Originally the territory extended from the Atlantic Ocean westward for an indefinite distance beyond the Delaware River, and from Nova Francia (Canada) on the north to Virginia on the south. Soon afterward the English began colonizing southern New England and the eastern half of Long Island. New Netherland was brought to the attention of Europeans by Hudson's discovery of its "Great River" in 1609, when he was in the employ of the Dutch East India Company and captain of the *Halve Maen* (Half-Moon), a *yacht* which flew the Dutch flag. New Netherland was visited by Dutch sailors in 1610, and its waters explored and its coastline charted by Dutch mariners during the following decade.

The States General made this territory—theirs they believed by right of discovery and exploration—into a Province and granted it the use of an earl's coat of arms. In 1621, they put its management into the hands of the Chartered West India Company (hereafter called the Company), subject to their jurisdiction. Through the Company's efforts and at its expense, Europeans settled in the Province from 1624 until 1664. Sporadically they sent furs, timber, and grain to the warehouse in Amsterdam.

During these forty years, England watched Holland's activities in New Netherland with an angry eye, and she frequently let the States General know that Hollanders were occupying her lands without her permission. She declared often and vociferously that the territory belonged to her because her mariners, the Cabots, had sailed along its coast in 1497-98. (She neglected to take into consideration the fact that the Cabots were Italians, not English, even though she claimed that Hudson, an Englishman, had no right to make discoveries for foreign nations.) Finally, Charles II gave New Netherland to his brother James, Duke of York and Albany, who in 1664 sent a squadron of four frigates under the command of Colonel Richard Nicolls to seize New Amsterdam, seat of New Netherland's government.

When the surrender of the city was demanded, Director-General Petrus Stuyvesant stubbornly refused to acquiesce, although Fort Amsterdam was in no condition to withstand a siege; it was undermanned and its magazine contained less than 2,000 pounds of powder, much of it not fit to use. Its chief gunner reported that if firing were begun in the morning, the supply of ammunition would be exhausted by evening. The New Amsterdam burghers begged that their city be turned over to the enemy without resistance, to prevent bloodshed and destruction of property. Their valiant and obstinate Director-General, ever loyal to the Company, refused their earnest pleadings. Finally, two British warships anchored broadside to the fort and British marines with lighted punk in their hands stood beside their guns ready to fire. Then, and then only, did the obdurate Stuyvesant consent to surrender. The terms of capitulation were drawn up at his home on the Bowery (*bouwerij*) by both his and Nicolls' commissioners, signed by them, and by Nicolls and Stuyvesant. On the morning of Monday, September 8, 1664, the last and most efficient of New Netherland's six governors led his little garrison of soldiers out of Fort Amsterdam and "with all the honors of war" marched them down Beaver Street to board the *Gideon*, then ready to sail for Holland.

British soldiers entered the fort, lowered the Company's flag and raised the Union Jack in its place. The Province thereby was made a colony of Great Britain. The territory, which Hudson had discovered for the Dutch, was called New York, and little New Amsterdam became the City of New York. Other communities throughout the Province were given English names or had their Dutch names anglicized.

Nine years later, England and Holland were again at each other's throats. In July, 1673, a Dutch fleet of between eighteen and twenty-three warships commanded by Captain Cornelis Evertsen and Jacob Benckes dropped anchor in New York Bay. On August 9th, the city surrendered without putting up a fight, and English soldiers departed "with colors flying and drums beating." The Province again became New Netherland, but the city's name was changed to New Orange. This restoration, however, was short-lived. On February 9, 1674, the Treaty of Westminster was signed, and under its provisions Holland received Surinam in South America, and England regained the Dutch possessions on the Continent of North America. Although Dutch rule there was ended forever, Dutch influence lasted for generations.

The descendants of the Dutch settlers continued to build houses in the Dutch style well into the first quarter of the 19th century. They retained the use of the Dutch language, at least among themselves, despite the efforts of the government to introduce English as the common tongue. English was not generally adopted by Dutch churches in their services until 1766, and then only in the City of New York. Dutch was always used in conducting the services in the Flatbush Church until 1824 when "the pastor of Flatbush," the Reverend Martinus Schoonmaker, passed away.

In 1844, at the last service that was held in the Middle Dutch Church of New York, the Reverend Doctor Thomas De Witt pronounced the benediction in Dutch, at a time when some of his colleagues were still giving lectures in that language. As late as 1866, Anne Rolff, wife of John Rutger Planten, Consul-General from The Netherlands to the Port of New York, wrote this to her sister in Amsterdam:

"The Dutch language has been handed down from parents to children and sometimes as far as the fifth generation. This is certainly proof of great love for their native country. I personally have observed the above very often in New Jersey where my brother was settled. A great many descendants of the Dutch live in that neighborhood. And it is a fact that one out of ten people will be able to understand you although it is not exactly our civilized Dutch that they speak. It is more like a countrified dialect, i.e., like the dialect our farmers speak. However it is strong evidence of the retaining element which is such a peculiar token of our national character."— *From a letter owned by Marguerite Planten Trull (Mrs. Frank), granddaughter of the writer.*

According to Agnes Scott Smith, writing in the *New York Folklore Monthly* for August, 1946, a large portion of the people of Hurley, New York, were speaking Dutch in 1878 "in preference to heavily accented English, at least when conversing among themselves." In the first decade of the 20th century, Cornelius Schoonmaker (1823-1912), living in the Flatbush section of Brooklyn where he was known among his intimates as Cobe, now and then lapsed into the tongue of his forebears, and his wife sang Dutch lullabies to their great-grandchildren. At that late date, a querulous child was said to be *krankie*, a tin dipper was called a *blikke*, and a grandmother, *grootje*. My own great-aunt, who died in 1925 and whose name was Sarah, was always called Sauchie, a corruption of *Saatje*, little Sarah.

Many of the quotations used in the following pages are from the *Journal of a Voyage to New York in* 1679-80. This was discovered by the Honorable Henry A. Murphy, United States Minister to The Hague, translated into English and edited by him for the Long Island Historical Society, which published it in 1867. The voyage was made by two Labadists of Wiewerd in Friesland, Jasper Dankers and Peter Sluyter. It was Dankers who wrote the Journal.

Finally, something should be said about the variations in spellings, which many readers will notice. This comes from an attempt to use the correct, or contemporary, form of a name at the time referred to. This applies not only to the names of towns and places, but also to family names as they have evolved over the generations. A special word should be said about the patronymic suffixes, -se, -sen, and -sz.; they all mean "son of——" and follow the form most often used by the person named.

The Chartered Towns
IN THE PROVINCE OF NEW NETHERLAND

DUTCH NAME	DATE OF CHARTER	ENGLISH NAME
Beverwyck including Fort Orange	1652	Albany
Bergen	1661	Part of Jersey City
Boswyck	1661	Bushwick
Breukelen	1644	Brooklyn
Esopus, Wiltwyck	1661	Kingston
Heemstede	1646	Hempstead
Midwout, Vlakkebos	1653	Flatbush
Middelburg	1652	Newtown
Nieu Amersfoort (settled 1638)	1657	Flatlands
Nieu Amstel	1657	New Castle
Nieu Haarlem	1660	Harlem
Nieu Utrecht (settled 1657)	1661	New Utrecht
Rustdorp	1656	Jamaica
s'Gravensande	1645	Gravesend

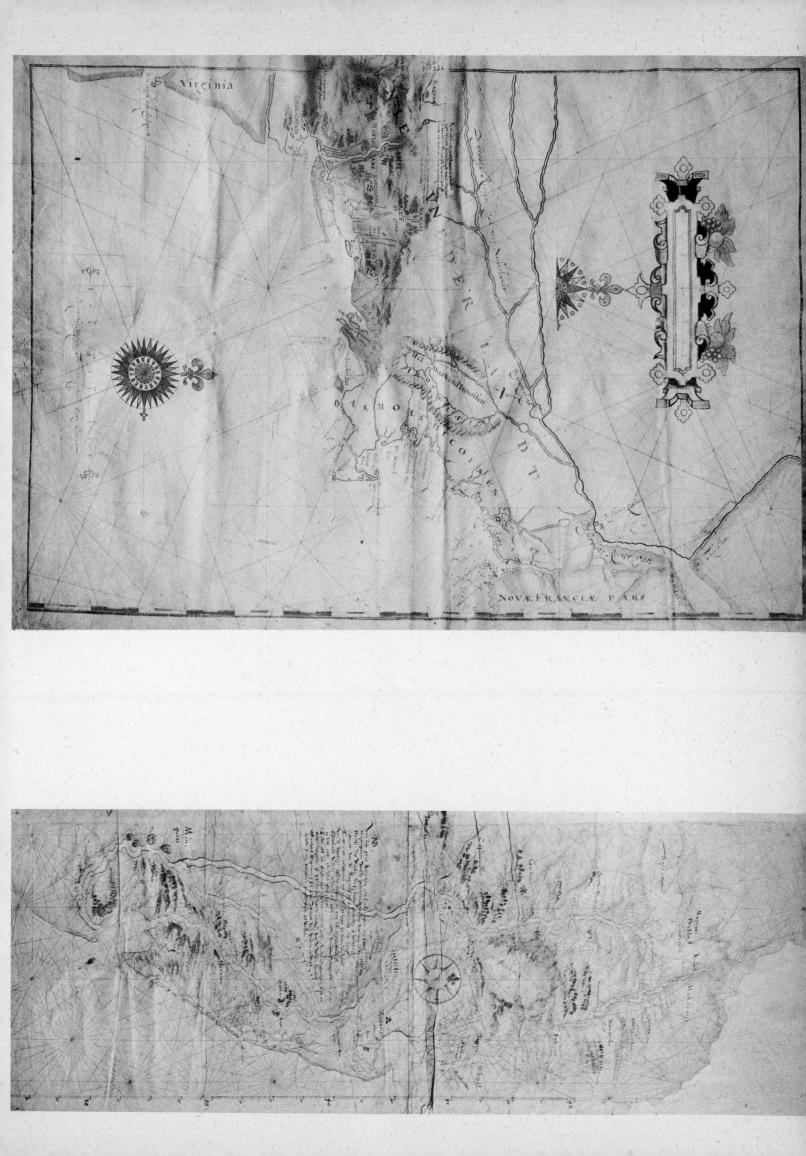

MANATVS
Gelegen op de Noot
Riuier

Noort River

Staten Eylant.

THREE EARLY MAPS OF NEW NETHERLAND

§1. *Block's Map*, also called the First Figurative Map, is painted in gold and colors on vellum. It was reproduced in 1635 by Willem Jansz. Blaeu in his World Atlas, and it is now in the Royal Archives, The Hague. It was lent by the Dutch Government to the Museum of the City of New York in the 1940's. This was the first map to show Manhattan and Long Island as islands, to use the name "Nieu Nederlandt," and to call the island off Rhode Island "Adriaen Blox Eylandt" (Block Island).

(Museum of the City of New York)

§2. *The Second Figurative Map* was drawn by Cornelis Hendricksen in 1616 on paper three feet long. It is in the Royal Archives, The Hague, and was lent to the Museum of the City of New York in the 1940's. It shows Fort Nassau on the upper Hudson and names the point of land at the entrance to New York Bay "Sandt Hoek," for the first time on a map.

(Museum of the City of New York)

§3. *The Manatus Map*, "Manhattan Lying on the North River," is in colors and is mounted on a canvas 24 7/16 inches by 17 1/16 inches. Made about 1760, it is a copy of a map drawn in 1639, probably by Andries Hudde, New Netherland's first surveyor-general. It is supposed to have been owned late in the 17th century by Hulst and Van Keuren, a famous publishing firm of Amsterdam. It was bought at a sale in 1887 by Henry Harrisse, "distinguished Americanist," who showed it at the Paris Columbia Exhibition of Maps and Globes in 1892 and then willed it to the Library of Congress, which received it in 1916. The inset contains the names of the property holders in the neighborhood of Manhattan Island.

(Library of Congress)

CHAPTER ONE

Fifty Years of Dutch Dominion

N NOVEMBER, 1613, Sir Thomas Dale and Captain Samuel Argall, on their return to Jamestown, Virginia, from a voyage to Acadia, reported that they had landed on "Manhattes Isle in Hudson's River, where they found four houses built, and a pretended Dutch Governour . . .who kept trading boats and was trucking with the Indians." The governor was undoubtedly Adriaen Block, skipper of the *Tiger*, who, together with Captain Hendrick Christiaensen in command of the *Fortune*, arrived at the mouth of the Hudson in the late spring or early summer of 1613. Christiaensen went to explore the river while Block anchored his vessel off Manhattan Island, which, by that time, Dutch sailors were calling "the Manhattes."

According to a 1613 Dutch record, the *Tiger* caught fire and burned. Block salvaged what he could and built a small *yacht* which he named the *Onrust* (Restless). She was 44 1/2 feet long, 11 1/2 feet wide, and had a 33-foot keel. As far as is known, she was the first vessel built by Europeans in New York waters.

Block went exploring in her, mapping and recording much that he saw. While cruising through Long Island Sound, he found that the Indians' *Paumanacke* (long land) was not part of the mainland but actually an island; he named it "Long Island." He discovered the Connecticut River, which he called the *Fresch Rivier*, and after sailing up it for some distance returned to the Sound. He rounded Point Judith and went along the Massachusetts coast as far north as Nahant harbor.

In the meantime, Christiaensen had sailed up the Hudson until he reached a small island off its west bank about 150 miles from its mouth. On it were the ruins of a stone fort that French sailors had been building in 1540 when a freshet flooded them out. Known as Castle Island, the land is now entirely under water opposite Albany, New York. Christiaensen replaced the ruins with a redoubt that he surrounded by an 18-foot moat and mounted with two Breteuil cannons and eleven swivel guns. He named the fort Nassau in honor of William the Silent's son Maurice, Prince of the House of Nassau, who at that time was Stadtholder of Holland. Leaving ten or twelve men to hold the fort for the Dutch and to procure beaver, otter, and other furs from the Indians, Christiaensen went on cruising in the *Fortune*. In the summer of 1614 he met Block off Cape Cod.

Block put Cornelis Hendricksen, possibly his *onder schipper* (first mate), in command of the *Restless* and returned on the *Fortune* to Amsterdam. When he reached the city in October, 1614, a beautifully painted map was made from his charts and reports and given to the States General. Hendricksen sailed the *Restless* as far south as Chinecoteaque Bay, and up the Delaware River, then called South River by the Dutch, until he reached the mouth of the Schuylkill (Hidden Creek), so named by sailors because they had come upon it unexpectedly. Like Block, Hendricksen drew maps and wrote reports which were presented to the States General after his return to Holland in August, 1616.

In 1621, a group of influential Dutch merchants was given permission by the States General to organize the Chartered West India Company, a corporation that was not only to have charge of the Dutch possessions in the New World but also to act as "a military arm of the state." It consisted of five chambers of directors, each of which had headquarters in its own community. The Amsterdam Chamber was entrusted with the colonizing and managing of New Netherland.

If they had not already done so, the Amsterdam Directors began at once to make preparations for sending forth settlers. They rented a building on Haarlem Street, Amsterdam, for their headquarters, built or chartered vessels for the transportation of people and cargoes, engaged a *ziekentrooster* (comforter-of-the-sick), and advertized for men and women desirous of moving to America.

By the winter of 1623-24, the Company's yacht *Mackeral* was in New Netherland waters; by spring, probably May, of 1624, its *New Netherland* and *Unity* had arrived at the mouth of the Hudson. Adriaen Jorise Thienpont skippered the *Unity*. "A man with one eye or with a film over his eye," Captain Cornelis Jacobse May (Mey), was in command of the *New Netherland*. Both men had been in the Province previously. May, who had given his name to New Jersey's cape, was made Director of New Netherland, and Thienpont Vice-Director, before they sailed from Amsterdam.

In that first group of colonists was a young woman, eighteen or nineteen years old, named Catalyntje Rapalje. She was the daughter of Jeronimus Trico of Pry and the wife of Joris Jansen Rapalje, also an immigrant. Many years after her arrival, Catalyntje made a deposition in which she told where the colonists settled. She said, "They sent two families and six men to harford (*sic*) River (the Connecticut), two families and eight men to the Delaware River, eight men were left at Manhattan to

HET WEST INDISCH HUYS

§4. The West India Company's House as seen from the *Oude Schans* is shown here in an engraving on copper. The building stood on the Rapenberg Quay in Amsterdam with three gables facing the harbor and three the *Oude Schans*, a canal street running past the Montelbaans Tower. It was originally built to serve as the Company's warehouse, but, later, the building was also utilized as the Company's headquarters from the time the Dutch lost Brazil in 1654 until the Company finally was dissolved in 1674.

(Museum of the City of New York)

take possession and ye rest of ye passengers went with ye ship up as far as Albany, which they then called Fort Orangie." She added a fact, hardly worth repeating, that four of the women who had sailed with her were married on shipboard.

It may well be that the group which went to the Delaware were the men who established Fort Nassau, built about that time at the mouth of Timber Creek, a site now in Gloucester County, New Jersey. Fort Nassau on Castle Island had been destroyed by flood waters in 1617 and its garrison moved to a place on the mainland which the Indians called *Tawasenthe*, "heap of dead men's bones." There the colonists of 1624 erected Fort Orange, naming it for Holland's unselfish hero, William of Orange. Orange was a principality in northeast France ruled by the House of Nassau.

"They forthwith put spade to the ground and began to plant, and before the yacht *Mackeral* sailed (on August 9th) their grain was nearly as high as a man," was the report sent to the Amsterdam Directors.

Captain May returned to Holland in the autumn, and Willen Verhulst arrived in the Province early in 1625 as its second Director. Verhulst brought with him the Company's engineer, Cryn Fredericksz. As he had been ordered, with the engineer's help, he chose a place "most suitable for the establishing of permanent settlement." It was on Manhattan Island, and its selection was Verhulst's only contribution to the Province.

He was followed by Peter Minuit, a Huguenot from Wesel in Westphalia and a man in his mid-forties, who was "dark-eyed, of robust form and brusque manner, but of sound principle and practical tact." Between August 9 and September 23, 1626, he bought Manhattan's 22,000 acres from the Indians for merchandise valued at 60 guilders, traditionally worth $24.00. Then leaving only a handful of men at the outlying forts, Minuit summoned the colonists to Manhattan Island in order to strengthen Fort Amsterdam, which was being erected on its southern tip. Although he had been considered by the Company worthy of the title of Director-General of New Netherland, within seven years Minuit was called back to Amsterdam to answer charges against his conduct in office.

Wouter Van Twiller, a twenty-five-year-old clerk in the Company's employ, superseded him. Van Twiller was the nephew of Kiliaen Van Rensselaer, a wealthy pearl and diamond merchant and one of the Company's most influential members. He arrived at New Amsterdam in April, 1633, and shortly thereafter began buying large tracts of land from the Indians, supposedly for the Company but actually in his own name. In 1638 he was ordered back to Holland to explain his real estate activity.

His successor, Willem Kieft, had a bad reputation. He had been a merchant who had gone bankrupt. He also had "had his portrait affixed to the gallows," a custom of that time. Kieft had appropriated part of the money entrusted to him when he went to ransom

§5. The seal of New Netherland was designed in Holland, adopted by the Company on December 28, 1630, and sent to New Amsterdam to be used on the legal documents of the province. It consisted of a beaver (symbol of New Netherland's source of wealth) proper on a small shield enclosed by wampum and applied to a larger shield. The crest of an earl's crown signified that the territory was a province of The Netherlands. The Latin words mean Seal of New Netherland.
(*Museum of the City of New York*)

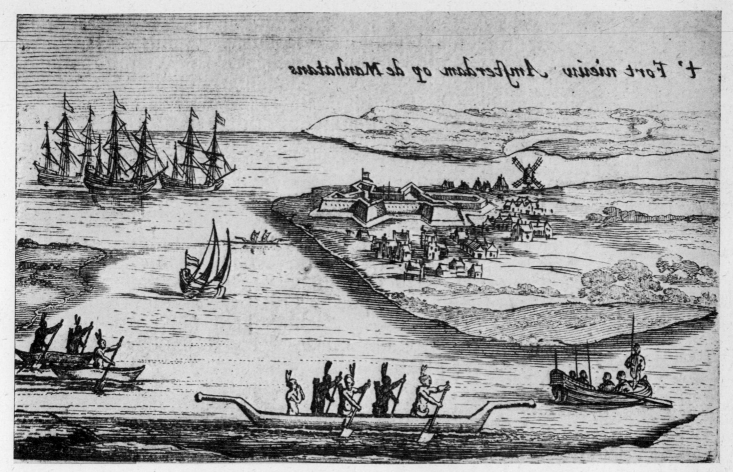

§6. The Hartger's View, the earliest known picture of New Amsterdam, is an engraving 4 1/2 inches by 3 1/4 inches. It is from a sketch made between 1626 and 1628, possibly by the Company's engineer, Cryn Fredericksz., and is largely anticipatory, for the fort was built with only four bastions. (The picture is reversed here to correspond with the topography of Manhattan Island and its surrounding territory.) The engraving was published in Amsterdam in 1651 by Joost Hartgers in his *Beschrijvinge van Virginie, Nieu Nederlandt, Nieu Englandt, Bermudas en St. Christoffel.* (*New-York Historical Society*)

Christians from the Turks and left a number of them in captivity. A quarrelsome, dictatorial man, he was highly unpopular in New Netherland, and he treated the Indians with such cruelty that they retaliated by killing the colonists on the outlying plantations and burning all the buildings. After nine years in office, Kieft also was recalled. Taking with him the fortune he had made in the Province and "some very valuable maps," he sailed for Holland on the *Princess* in September, 1647, and was drowned when the vessel was wrecked off the coast of Wales in an autumn storm.

Petrus Stuyvesant, on board the *Princess* when she arrived at New Amsterdam on May 11, 1647, was the most efficient of New Netherland's six governors. After an administration of seventeen years, he was in office at the time of the surrender.

While these officials were coming and going, the Company's vessels were carrying colonists and cargoes to New Netherland, and settlements were being made from the banks of the Connecticut all the way south to the shores of the Delaware. Several patroonships were also started, but only one endured: Rensselaerswyck, Kiliaen Van Rensselaer's great estate of 700,000 acres, forty-eight miles wide, and extending for twenty-four miles along both sides of the upper Hudson. The Dutch, following the Company's explicit directions, always paid the Indians for the land they obtained. But the red men, unversed in the rules of European civilization, did not realize until it was too late that they were parting forever with their fields and woods and streams for such paltry articles as glass beads, little mirrors, awls, beer, and red coats.

Fort Amsterdam, first called Fort Nieu Amsterdam, was laid out on the southern end of Manhattan Island, and houses were built close to its walls and along the strand of the East River. A church was also erected, as well as taverns and a city hall. The entire community was named Nieu Amsterdam.

Towns were established in all parts of the Province of New Netherland. Nieu Amersfoort, Breukelen, Midwout, Nieu Utrecht, and Boswyck were founded on the west end of Long Island. Haarlem was settled at the northern end of Manhattan Island. Bergen was established in what is now the State of New Jersey, and Nieu Amstel sprang up on the west bank of the Delaware. A small settlement was made on Staten Island, and others were made at Arresack, Ahasimus, Communipaw, Hoboken, Weehawken, and Paulus Hook on the west side of New York Bay; at the "Flats" (Schenectady) where the Binne Kill meets the Mohawk River; at Adriaen van der Donck's *Colen Donck* (Yonkers, New York); and on Cornelis Antonissen van der Sluyck's and Jonas Bronck's lands along the Kaaterskill.

Fort Beversrede was built at the junction of the Delaware and Schuylkill rivers; Fort Casimir, around which grew the settlement of Nieu Amstel (now New Castle), was erected on the west bank of the Delaware; and a blockhouse was constructed at Naaman's near the present Claremont, Delaware.

The House of Good Hope, in the vicinity of the present Hartford, Connecticut, was erected as a trading post. Another was set up on Kievitt's Hoek at the mouth of the Connecticut, and a farmhouse or two were built at Oostdorp (Greenwich, Connecticut). However, all of these settlements were seized by New Englanders a number of years before 1664. New Englanders, with the permission of both Kieft and Stuyvesant, also settled Gravesend, Newtown, Jamaica, and Hempstead on the west end of Long Island, and these settlements were supposedly under Dutch jurisdiction.

Without permission, Swedes built Fort Elsinborg on the east bank of the Delaware, Fort Christina on Christina Creek, and a fort and house on Tinicum Island in the Delaware. They named the territory they occupied New Sweden, its first governor being Johan Printz. They even had the temerity to seize Fort Casimir, which they renamed Trinity. But, when Stuyvesant sailed up the Delaware in 1655 with seven warships bristling with cannon and carrying between 600 and 700 armed men, they surrendered without firing a shot, and thereafter lived as peaceful citizens of New Netherland.

At the time of the surrender, exclusive of the Indians, there were 10,000 souls, more or less, living in New Netherland. This population consisted not only of natives of The Netherlands, who naturally predominated, but also Britishers, Flemings, Germans, Huguenots, Jews, Italians, Scandinavians, Walloons, Waldensians from the Piedmont, Negroes brought as slaves from the Gold Coast of Africa, and the American-born offspring of these different nationalities.

They spoke Dutch as their common language, attended the services of the Dutch Reformed Church, sent their children to Dutch schools, followed the manners and customs of the Low Countries, and lived under the old Roman civil laws as administered in Amsterdam and throughout Holland. They posted the arms of Holland on newly acquired lands and flew the orange, white, and blue horizontally striped flag, with GWC, for *Geoctroyerde Westindische Compagnie* (Chartered West India Company), on its white stripe. They were governed by the Director-General appointed by the Company and his Council.

Each chartered town had its *schepen* (magistrate) and *schout* (constable) to see that order was maintained and laws obeyed. The duty of the *schout* was to prevent disorder, investigate crimes, seize suspects, present them to the *schepen*, and execute the sentence imposed on them. If capital punishment seemed to be needed, the prisoner was sent to Amsterdam for the Company's decision as to what should be done.

New Amsterdam was the only city in the Province, a bustling, prosperous little community which was given municipal government on February 12, 1653. A few days later, its two burgomasters and five *schepen* held their first session in the City Tavern, which was thereafter the *Stadt Huys* (City Hall). The city's other officials were the *schout*, preacher, teacher, secretary, court messenger, and dog-catcher. Their salaries were paid, supposedly, with money obtained from excise licenses.

§7 (BELOW). *The seal of New Amsterdam was designed in Holland and sent by the Company*
to Stuyvesant, who gave it to the magistrates of the city on December 8, 1654. It consisted
of a silver shield with a vertical band charged with three diagonal crosses (from the
arms of Amsterdam). The crest is a beaver, symbol of the fur trade. The Latin
words mean Seal of Amsterdam in New Netherland. The colors, orange,
white and blue, are those of the Prince's flag, the standard of the West
India Company with its monogram in black, on the white stripe.
The monogram stands for the Geoctroyerde Westindische
Compagnie (The Chartered West India Company).

(MUSEUM OF THE CITY OF NEW YORK)

§8. These charred timbers of an ancient vessel were found in 1904 by work-men digging the subway in lower Manhattan. City historians believed the vessel to be Block's *Tiger*. James A. Kelly, official historian of Kings County, salvaged the part of the hull which is now in the Marine Gallery, Museum of the City of New York. The remainder lies buried beneath the junction of Greenwich and Dey Streets.

(*Museum of the City of New York*)

§9. The Taler, a silver coin made in Overyssel, The Nether-lands, went into circulation in 1614, the year that Block, Christiaensen, and Hendricksen were exploring New Nether-land waters.

(*Museum of Moneys of the World, Chase Manhattan Bank*)

§10. "Nieu Amsterdam" is an engraving on copper measuring 9 5/7 inches by 7 1/8 inches. It may have been made about 1643, but little is known about its origin. It has been said to resemble the work of Peter van der Berge, and it may have been in one of the 17th or 18th century collections of Dutch engravings. It belonged to the late Isaac Newton Phelps Stokes, who showed it in his *Iconography of Manhattan Island*.

§11. New Netherland's official coins were the stivers and guilders used in The Netherlands; twenty stivers in one guilder. More often beaver pelts and Indian wampum were the media of exchange. The pelts were given as a whole or cut into pieces. Wampum, called seawan by the Dutch, consisted of tiny purple and white pierced beads made from the inner sides of clam shells, the colored beads being the more valuable. Much of the wampum was made on the western end of Long Island.

(*Numismatic Society of America*)

§12. (OPPOSITE) This water color of Peter Stuyvesant's pear tree was painted in June, 1866, by Abram Hosier for the New-York Historical Society. The tree, when a sapling, was brought to New Amsterdam in 1647 by Stuyvesant and planted on Bowery No. 1, which later became his property. The tree stood on the northeast corner of Third Avenue and 13th Street in New York until it was blown down in 1873. It last blossomed in 1867. Its last pear, withered but still on its branch with a few dried leaves, was kept as a treasure in a shadow-box and shown at the Dutch Colonial Heirloom Exhibition.

(*New-York Historical Society*)

June. 1866.

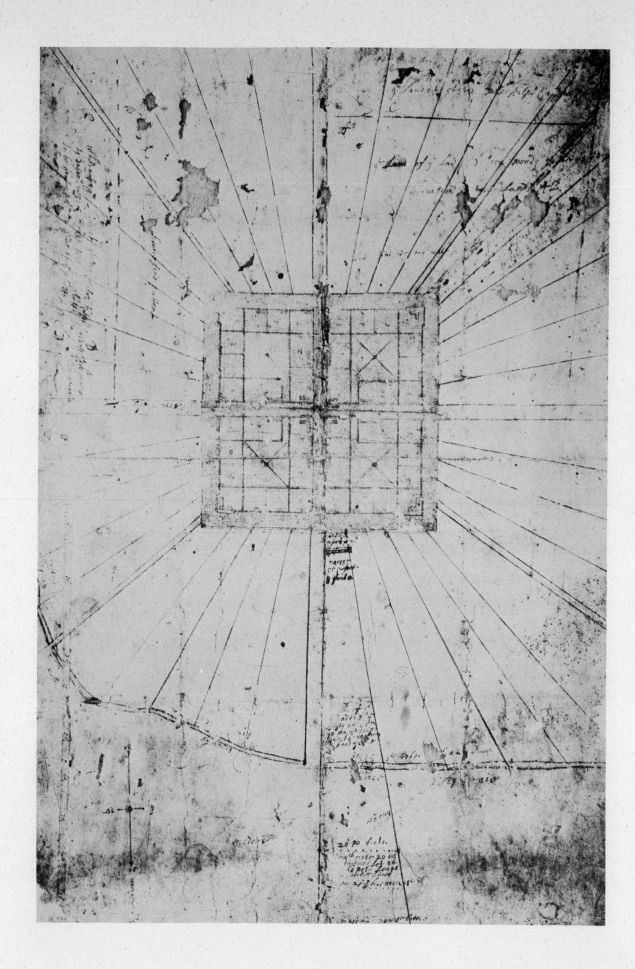

§14. Called the Van Rensselaer Cannon, although it bears the Company's monogram, this cannon was made in 1630 by Assuerus Koster, Amsterdam's famous gun and bell founder, and probably was sent to Fort Orange that same year. In 1663, at the outbreak of the Second Esopus War, Rensselaerswyck demanded the return of a cannon previously lent to the fort, and this one was probably sent by mistake. It remained in the Van Rensselaer family until 1939, when it was added to the historical collection of the New York State Museum.

(New York State Museum)

§13. (OPPOSITE) A plan of the Town of Gravesend, Long Island, settled in 1643, is in the County Clerk's Office of Kings County, New York. On its back is a statement made by John Emans, clerk of Gravesend, 1688-1705, who was acquainted with the plan "from personal or direct information." It says, "I would not any to Admire this plote nor for to thinke it was Lade down by one wo (who) understood it not. For he that dus thinke so, the plote ded not know. Althoughe not founded by ye Grounds of tre (three), yet being ingenus therein he ded it, but only by suposition for after memry. 1694 September 29."

(James A. Kelly, Official Historian of Kings County, N. Y.)

§15. This lock and key, made in Holland, were used in the powder magazine at Fort Orange, which stood approximately on the site in Albany that was later called Steamboat Square and is now occupied by the city's railroad station.

(Albany Institute of History and Art)

§16. "New Amsterdam Now New York" is called the Schenk View of the city because it was first shown in Petri Schenk's *View of One Hundred Cities*, published in 1702. It is an engraving on copper 9 3/8 inches by 7 1/16 inches, showing the city as it looked shortly after its recapture by the Dutch in 1673.

(*New York Public Library*)

§17. Washington Irving, "America's first internationally recognized author," used this tin and wood weathercock on a gable of Sunnyside, his home in Tarrytown, New York, facetiously claiming that it originally topped New Amsterdam's *Stadt Huys*. Before his death in November, 1859, he gave it to the St. Nicholas Society of the City of New York, which now has it on loan with the New-York Historical Society.

(New-York Historical Society)

CHAPTER TWO
The Colonists

Plates 18-39

§18. Petrus Stuyvesant, as he usually signed his name, was the last Director-General of New Netherland. He was intelligent, efficient, and always loyal to the Company, but dictatorial and fiery-tempered. Son of the Reverend Balthazar Stuyvesant, he was born in 1601 or 1602 in Scherpenzel, Friesland, and attended the University of Francker. In 1635 he went as the Company's supercargo to an island off the coast of Brazil. From there he wrote asking to be promoted to an office "according to my capacity," and he was made Governor of Curacao. He wrote, "I did not succeed as well as I had hoped, no small impediment being the loss of my right leg which was removed by a tough ball. To tell of everything at length my illness does not permit." After a sickness of 18 months, he left for Holland. He sailed on the *Milkmaid,* which was wrecked off the Irish coast. He then made his way to his sister's home at Alphen near Leid‑ in Holland, where he was betrothed to her sister-in-law, Judith Bayard. They were married in the Walloon church in Breda, August 13, 1645. Having been appointed Governor-General of New Netherland, he sailed with his young wife on the *Princess* and arrived at New Amsterdam in May, 1647. After th‑ surrender, he was summoned to Holland to explain why he ha‑ capitulated without firing a shot. He then returned to New Amsterdam where he spent the rest of his days as a private citizen. He died in 1672. His portrait, in oils on a canvas 21 1/2 inches by 17 1/2 inches, was painted, probably in the 1660's, b‑ an unidentified artist. *(New-York Historical Society*

CHAPTER TWO
The Colonists

"THE DUTCH were a small people who founded a great republic under great discouragement," wrote John Fisk in his *History of the American Colonies*. They were a brave people who fought Philip of Spain's powerful armies and cruel Alva in order to have political freedom and religious liberty. Determined and industrious, they struggled for generations with the tides of the North Sea for much of the land on which they live.

After their delivery from Spain, their *Patria* (as some of the colonists called their homeland) was a country "where political and religious freedom (were) highly prized, popular education was nearly universal, and regard for law and order was most profound; where the rewards of industry were widely shared, the necessities of life abundantly secured and the blessings of civilization equally diffused."

Such was the inheritance of the Dutch people who settled New Netherland. According to Chancellor Kent in an address before the New-York Historical Society in 1828, the Dutch colonists were "grave, temperate, firm, persevering men who brought (to New Netherland) the industry and simplicity, the integrity and the bravery of their Belgic sires." They were peaceful and prudent, hospitable in an unostentatious way, kind and considerate to strangers, and little given to either boasting or grumbling. There was a saying among those who had dealings with them in the mid-19th century that a Dutchman's word was as good as his bond.

However, they were apt to be deliberate and phlegmatic and slow to move, as General Howe discovered to his dismay. During the American Revolution he wrote to George III, "I can do nothing with the Dutch population (of the Hudson Valley). I can neither buy them with money nor conquer them with fear."

The colonists came from very different backgrounds. Many were of simple peasant stock while others were members of highly educated and cultured families. Governor Francis Lovelace of New York wrote to his king, James II, in 1688, "Many of these people have the breeding of courts and I cannot understand how such was acquired."

The majority of the colonists were farmers with a trade on the side. Many worked for the Company as officials, agents, soldiers and servants, surgeons and midwives. A few were pastors of the Dutch Reformed Church, comforters-of-the-sick, teachers, and surveyors. Others were bakers, blacksmiths, brewers, carpenters, glaziers, laborers, merchants, sailors, traders, and tavern-keepers. A few, the *booschlopen* (wood runners), spent their time in the forests trapping and trading for furs with the Indians.

Issac de Forest, a brewer, was also the official dog-catcher. Gillis de Mandeville was a liquor dealer. Jan Strycker is listed as an armorer, although there is no record of his work or of his having done such work. Adriaen van der Donck, a lawyer, wrote *A Description of New Netherland.* Nicasius de Sille, Schout-Fiscal of the Province and town clerk of Nieu Utrecht, was the author of the *History of the First Beginnings of Nieu Utrecht.* Jacob Steendam published his *Den Distelvink* (thistle finch) and some other poems in 1649-50, and in *The Praise of New Netherland,* he spoke of the Province as "New Netherland, thou noblest spot on earth."

There were a few painters in the Province, among whom the Duyckincks, Evert and Gerrit, were the most important. There was also Jacob Strycker, but what purports to be his work has never been authenticated. On October 12, 1663, "the wife of Hendrick Coutrie" was asked by the burgomasters of New Amsterdam if she had purchased the burgher right (license to carry on a trade). She replied that it had been given to her husband by the Director-General. When asked by one of the burgomasters whether he had given something for it, she answered that he had painted a portrait of "his honor" and drawn pictures of his sons. At that time, "Hendrick Coutrie" was a merchant living with his wife in Nieu Amstel (New Castle). According to a Leiden church record, "Hendrick Couterie, *schilder* (painter), and Lysbeth Copejn were married on June 4, 1648." He was a grosgrain manufacturer and a member of St. Lucas Guild. A short time after his marriage, it was noted that he had left Leiden. There is no proof, as is sometimes claimed, that he painted the only portrait of Stuyvesant known to exist, the one owned by the New-York Historical Society.

§20. The portrait from which this photograph was made was printed many years ago on a leaflet, next to one of *Domine* Bogardus and a genealogical chart, with the name "Anneke W. Jansen-Bogardus" below it.

Annetje, rather than Anneke, Jans is known in New York history as the owner of a 162-acre farm on the North River which Queen Anne gave to Trinity Church Corporation, and for which Annetje's descendants fought in the New York courts until the State Legislature, in the early years of the 20th century, forbade such a suit.

Annetje was the daughter of Tryn Jonas, New Netherland's first official midwife. She married Roeloff Jans of Masterland and arrived with him at Rensselaerswyck in 1630, along with their daughters, Sara and Tryntje, and "another child born before in New Netherland." By 1636, they were living in New Amsterdam on the North River farm for which Roeloff had been given a deed. He died shortly thereafter, leaving her with four daughters and a son, Jan. Annetje married *Domine* Bogardus in 1638. After he was drowned, she wrote the Amsterdam Classis asking to be permitted to have her late husband's salary of 46 guilders monthly, as well as his annual board allowance of 160 guilders. She moved to Fort Orange, where she died in 1663, leaving her estate divided equally among her children, except the 1,000 guilders from the North River farm which were to go to Roeloff's offspring.

§19. Reverend Evardus Bogardus was the second *domine* to officiate in the Province. He arrived at New Amsterdam in April, 1633, on the *Soutberg* (Salt Mountain) with Wouter Van Twiller. His church was a large, barnlike building on *t' Water* (30 Pearl Street) until the Church in the Fort was erected. He had frequent quarrels with the New Netherland magistrates, often denouncing them from the pulpit. They charged him with drunkenness, meddling in others' affairs, and using bad language. In September, 1647, leaving his wife and sons Willem, Cornelis, Jonas, and Pieter in New Amsterdam, he sailed on the *Princess* for Holland to defend himself from the charges brought against him. He was drowned when the *Princess* was wrecked.

Bogardus was born in The Netherlands in 1607. He attended the University of Leiden, went as comforter-of-the-sick to Guinea, and was later ordained minister of the Reformed Church. He was sent to New Amsterdam, where in 1638 he married Annetje Jans, a widow with four children and a farm of 162 acres on the North River. At one time he owned a plot of ground on Maspat Kill, Long Island, which was called "Domine's Hook" for generations.

This portrait of him was owned by Robert Tappan, Brooklyn printer, on February 22, 1864, when it was exhibited at Brooklyn's Sanitary Fair and listed on page nine of its *Catalogue of Fine Arts, Relics and Curiosities* as "Evardus Bogardus painted on glass 240 years ago."

§21. The photograph shown above was given to the author in 1940 by the late Victor Hugo Palsitis of the New York Public Library. It is of a framed portrait in oils presented to the Library by a donor who claimed it was the likeness of New York's well-known Annetje Jans. It has "A. Jans 1684," painted to the right of the sitter. *The* Annetje Jans died in 1663.

(*New York Public Library*)

§22. Anna Marika (Stuyvesant) Bayard was a widow with three young
children when she arrived at New Amsterdam in 1647 with her brother and
his wife. She was well-educated, spoke English and French as well as she did
Dutch, and had "intelligence, refinement and solidity of thought and character." She is shown in the above painting with her husband, Samuel
Bayard, whom she married in 1638 in Amsterdam, at Alphen, their home
in Holland which they acquired in 1644.

   The painting, in oils on a wood panel 34 1/2 inches by 48 inches, is by
an unidentified artist and was probably done in 1644. It was taken to New
Amsterdam in 1647 and was hanging in Stuyvesant's Bowery Mansion,
then the home of Gerardus (1691-1777) and Judith (Bayard) Stuyvesant,
when seen by Eugene Pierre du Simitiere in July, 1768. Du Simitiere,
"Swiss naturalist, portraitist, painter, and art collector," was in America
collecting data on painting in the colonies. He wrote that Peter Stuyvesant's grandson, Gerardus, owned a painting, "a conversation piece, that
showed a landscape with two figures, some members of the family, tolerably
well done."

(New-York Historical Society)

§23. Nicholas William Stuyvesant, second son of the Director-General, was born in New Amsterdam in 1648. As he had no need to earn a living, he devoted his time to his church and to charitable works. He inherited the bulk of his father's large estate and went to live in the Bowery Mansion after the death of his mother. His first wife was Maria, daughter of William Beekman. After her death, he married Elizabeth, daughter of Barent Aertsz. van Slichtenhorst and the mother of his three children. His portrait, inscribed "Aetatis Sua 17 an° 1666," is painted in oils on canvas 36 inches by 25 5/8 inches by an unidentified artist.

§24. Cornelis Jacobse Van Steenwyck, wealthy trader, ship and real estate owner of New York, is supposed to have visited his sister in Haarlem, Holland, in 1667 or 1668, when this portrait of him was painted in oil on canvas by his brother-in-law, Jan Van Gooten.

Van Steenwyck first arrived in New Amsterdam from Haarlem prior to 1651, for at that time he had established his home and store on *t' Water* (27 Pearl Street). Seven years later he married Marguerite De Riemer, stepdaughter of *Domine* Drisius, and moved into a large double stone house on what is now the corner of Bridge and Whitehall Streets, where he lived in luxury until he died in 1684. Of his seven children, only his son Isaac (born in 1660) survived him. Cornelis was a *schepen* of the city and its burgomaster. In 1663, for the city's defense, he lent Stuyvesant 10,000 guilders on the Company's draft, backed by four brass cannons in the fort. He was also one of the commissioners to arrange terms for the surrender. Later he assured Nicolls that he would be a willing and obedient subject as long as the government remained in the hands of the English. Able to speak and understand English, Steenwyck was put on the Governor's Council, and in 1671, when Lovelace was absent from the city, he acted as temporary governor. Then, after the recapture of the city by the Dutch, he was Governor Colve's sole Councillor. When England regained possession, he was Mayor of New York for two terms. By his will, after providing amply for his wife and relations, he left his Manor of Fordham, in Westchester County, to the Dutch Church for the maintenance of its minister, "for which purpose it should always remain."

§25. Jacob Steendam, who called himself "a trader," was in New Netherland from early in 1649 until 1660. He owned various pieces of property in New Amsterdam, a plantation in Amersfoort (Flatlands), Long Island, and land on Maspat Kill, Long Island. His wife was Sara de Rosschou. They had a daughter, Vredgond, and sons, Samuel and Jacob, who were born in New Amsterdam and baptized in its church. Some years after Steendam had left New Netherland, he went to Batavia as a comforter-of-the-sick. He was governor of its orphan's house when he died in 1671.

Steendam was one of America's first poets. Born in 1616 in Enkhuysen, Holland, he began writing poetry at the age of twenty. In 1649-50, he published a book of verse, *Den Distelvink*. He continued writing while in New Netherland, where he exalted its natural beauties. Deeply interested in its affairs, he deplored the neglect of the Province by the home government and wrote *The Complaint of New Amsterdam to its Mother*. In "The Praise of New Netherland," he sang:

> *This is the land where milk and honey flow;*
> *Where wholesome herbs freely as thistles grow;*
> *The land where Aaron's Rod its buds doth show;*
> *A very Eden!*

§26. Jan Strycker was a farmer of Flatbush, Long Island, a *schepen* and patentee of the town, and its delegate to the Hempstead Convention. Although he is listed as an armorer, there is no mention of his work in the records. He was born in The Netherlands in 1617 and there married to Lambertje Seubering, the mother of his children. He emigrated from Ruinen in Drenthe in 1652 and had settled in Flatbush as early as 1654. After the death of Lambertje, he married Swantje, widow of Cornelis de Potter, and when again a widower, he took for his third wife, Teuntje Teunis, widow of Jacob Hellakers, the Nieu Utrecht carpenter. He died before 1697. His farm was on the present northeast corner of Flatbush and Church Avenues, Brooklyn.

The back of his portrait, which was painted by Jacobus Strycker in 1655, once bore the inscription: "Given to Altje by her father Jacobus Gerritsen Striker, who, himself, drew this likeness of his brother Jan." This was signed by Johannes Coerten Van Voorhees, nephew of Altje's husband, Abram Coerten Van Voorhees of Flatlands, Long Island.
(A. W. Mellon Educational and Charitable Fund, National Gallery)

§27 & 28. These portraits of Johan Printz and his wife are copies of paintings
in oil by an unknown artist in the vicarage of Bottnaryd, Smaland. They
were given in 1938 by a Printz descendant to the American Swedish Historical Museum.

Johan Bjornsson Printz (1592-1663) was born in Bottnaryd, Smaland, and
attended German universities. He spent some years in the Swedish army
before being sent to America in 1643, where for ten years he was "Governor
of New Sweden," a settlement made in New Netherland by the Swedes
without permission from the Dutch. "New Sweden" lasted until 1655,
when Stuyvesant demanded the surrender of its government. David
Pietersz. de Vries, a Dutch sea captain, visited Printz and noted in his *Korte
Historiael* that the Swede was "a wise man with a stature of more than four
hundred pounds." The Indians called him *Meschantz* (big belly).

This portrait of Printz's wife is, probably, of Maria von Linnestan, whom
he married after the death of his first wife in 1640 and before they sailed for
New Sweden in 1643. They made their home at Printz Hall, which was
built after a fire in 1646. It was their home until their return to Sweden in
1653.

(*American Swedish Historical Museum, Philadelphia*)

§29. Gerrit Duyckinck (1660 - *ca.* 1710) was the tenth and youngest child of Evert and Hendrickje (Simonse) Duyckinck of New Amsterdam. Like his father, he was "a limner, a painter, a glazier, a painter of glass, and a glass maker." He also took an interest in civic affairs, for he was an alderman of New York and captain of its militia. In 1688 he was made a Freeman of the city and later signed the petition for a ferry to Brooklyn. Of his eleven children, only his son Gerrit, called Gerardus, was a painter. This self-portrait, in oils on a wooden panel 30 inches by 25 inches, was painted in 1695.

Jasper Dankers, one of the Labadists, mentioned Gerrit in his *Journal of a Voyage to New York in 1679-80* in the following passage:

"They had a new church in Hysopis (Kingston, New York), of which the glass had been made and painted in the city by the father of our mate Evert Duiker, whose other son, Gerrit, did most of the work. This Gerrit Duiker has to take the glass to Hysopis . . . . He promised to teach me to draw."

(New-York Historical Society)

§30. Maria Duyckinck was the daughter of Christoffel Jansz.
Abeel and his wife Neeltje Jans Kroom. She was born in Albany
in 1666 and was married to Gerrit Duyckinck on July 16, 1683.
Her portrait, in oils on canvas 30 1/4 by 27 7/8 inches, was
painted by her husband, probably in the year of their marriage.
(New-York Historical Society)

§31. David Provoost, Jr., the son of David and Maragretta (Gillis) Provoost, was born in 1642 in New Amsterdam, probably in his father's farmhouse on the East River Road near where the ferry to Brooklyn was then, or later, established. He was baptized by *Domine* Bogardus in the newly erected Church of St. Nicholas, the Church in the Fort, in 1645. From 1694 to 1698 he was assessor of the Dock Ward, City of New York. His portrait was painted in oils on a wooden panel, 30 inches by 25 inches, about 1700 by an unidentified New York artist.

(New-York Historical Society)

§32. Mrs. Tryntje (Laurens) Provoost was born in Amsterdam, Holland, in 1650 and emigrated to New Amsterdam. In 1668 she was married by *Domine* Polhemus to David Provoost, Jr., in Flatbush. Her portrait was painted in oils on a wooden panel, 30 inches by 25 inches, about 1700 by an unidentified New York artist.

(New-York Historical Society)

§33. The Reverend Johannes Weeksteen was *domine* of the Kingston, New York, church from September 11, 1681, until his death on March 17, 1687. He was sent to the church at the request of his sister-in-law, widow of Reverend Laurentus van Gaasbeck, its late pastor, and was held in "great affection and love by his congregation." Born in 1638, Weeksteen was a Latin teacher living in Haarlem with his family when he was called to be examined for the ministry. He was so successful that he was unanimously given the degree of D.V.M. (Minister of God's Word). After being ordained by the laying on of hands, he was sent to Kingston where he was to have a "house, fuel and 600 bushels of wheat annually" in return for his services. His portrait, in oils on canvas, was painted by Mattys Mathieu, probably in Holland at the time of his ordination.

(Exhibition of Dutch Colonial Heirlooms)

§34. "Grootje Vas" is the name by which Elsje Rutgers is still affectionately known by some of her descendants. The daughter of Harmanus and Catherine Rutgers, she was born in 1674 in Albany, New York. On New Year's Day, 1694, she was married to David Davidse Schuyler, who was Mayor of Albany in 1705 and 1706. David died in 1715, leaving her with four sons and two daughters. After seven years of widowhood, she married *Domine* Vas, a widower, and went to live in the parsonage of the Kingston, New York, church. She was a widow again in 1752, and after that she moved to Rhinebeck, New York, where she died. She was never seen without her coif, of black velvet in winter and white linen in summer.

This portrait of her was painted in 1733, when she was fifty-nine, by Pieter Vanderlyn, husband of her stepdaughter. Its gold frame is thought to have been brought from Holland. This framed portrait was "lost" for years, but it was found in New Brunswick, New Jersey, by a Kingston antique dealer who sold it in 1936 to Grootje's descendant, Mrs. Theodore Delaporte. Mrs. Delaporte willed it to another descendant, Mrs. Harry H. Hill of Rhinebeck, and it is now in Winterthur.

(Winterthur Museum, Wilmington, Delaware)

§35. Reverend Ulpianus Van Sinderen was one of the last two preachers sent by the Classis of Amsterdam to New York. He was installed in 1746 as *domine* of the Church in Flatbush, Long Island, where he made his home for many years. With the help of another pastor, he had charge of the churches in the five Dutch towns on Long Island. He is said to have been "short of stature, very active, learned but deficient in sound judgment." Often he had word battles from the pulpit with members of his Flatbush congregation. Although he was in enemy territory from 1776 until 1783, no one ever doubted his patriotism.

He was living in Flatlands, Long Island, with one of his children in December, 1783, when he received a letter from the Consistory of the Flatbush Church, and he "burst into tears" on reading, "We need your services no longer." He was given an annual pension of fifty pounds until he died on July 23, 1796. He is buried in the graveyard of the Flatlands Church. Benjamin J. Lossing painted his portrait in water colors on paper in 1793, when he was 86 years old.

(*Long Island Historical Society*)

§36. Pau de Wandelaer was a member of a prosperous Albany and New York trading family. Nothing is known about him except that he lived in Albany. This portrait was painted about 1725, in oils on canvas 44 3/4 inches by 35 1/4 inches, by the Gansevoort Limner.

(*Albany Institute of History and Art*)

§37. "A Dutch Child of New Amsterdam" is the title of this painting, owned by Mrs. Katherine S. Davies, done by John Vanderlyn II about 1856. It is thought to have been copied from a portrait by Nicholas Vanderlyn, or, more probably, from the portrait of Helena Jansen Sleight of Kingston painted in 1700 by Pieter Vanderlyn.

(*Museum of the City of New York*)

§38. The portrait in oils pictured here was found in the walls of an old house being demolished in lower Manhattan. The names of the lovely little girl and of the artist who painted her are unknown.

(*Mrs. Reginald P. Rose, Oyster Bay, New York*)

§39. This portrait of Matthew Ten Eyck (at the oak), in oils on canvas 56 inches by 35 1/2 inches, was painted by Pieter Vanderlyn. It bears the inscription, "Geboren . . . Februarij A° 1728—Geschildert . . . A° 1733." (Born February, 1728, painted 1733) The sober-looking five-year-old of Hurley, New York, grew up to be a leading citizen of Ulster County, New York. He was quartermaster of its Troop of Horse prior to the Revolution. As President of the Village of Hurley, where he lived, he made a welcoming address to General Washington, who stopped at its tavern in 1782 on his way from West Point to Kingston. He died in 1809.

(Frick Art Reference Library, Collection of Mrs. Matthew Ten Eyck De Witt)

CHAPTER THREE
Religion in New Netherland

Plates 40-60

§40. The church pictured here was erected in Brooklyn in 1766 in the middle of the road to Jamaica (Fulton Street near its junction with Joralemon Street) on the site of the former, century-old Dutch Church. Its bell was the one sent by the Company in 1666 for the first church. This second building, demolished in 1807, was described as follows:

" . . . a large, square edifice with solid and very thick walls, plastered and whitewashed on every side up to the eaves . . . . The interior was plain, dark and very gloomy; so that in summer one could not see to read in it after four o'clock in the afternoon by reason of its small windows. These were six or eight feet above the floor, and filled with stained glass lights brought from Holland, representing vines loaded with flowers."

This painting of it, which was probably made
belonged to the late J. Duffield Prince of Br

Religion in New Netherland

A T THE time of the Reformation, the peoples of the Low Countries, desirous of following the Word of God as taught in the Bible, broke away from Roman Catholicism. They met in private places and called themselves "The Churches of The Netherlands under the Cross." Jan Arentsen started outdoor preaching in a large field near Hoorn in North Holland, which attracted thousands of listeners, and this started field-preaching in other parts of the country.

During these services, children were baptized, marriage ceremonies were performed, and collections were made for the poor. The Psalms, translated into Dutch from the French versions made by Marot and Beza from the original Hebrew, were sung with enthusiasm.

Because the leaders of these people could not meet safely in their own country to formulate rules for their church government, they attended the Synod of Wesel in 1568. While there, they accepted a confession of faith similar to that which John Calvin gave to his French churches. It was called the Belgic Confession because its author was Guido de Bes, a Belgian. In 1574, after Alva's departure from their country, Dutch religious leaders met in the Synod of Dort (Dordrect) where they adopted Protestantism as their national religion, the Belgic Confession of Faith, the Heidelberg Catechism, and a liturgy prepared by Peter Dathemus, a Protestant who had fled from Spanish persecution and settled in the Palatinate, at Frankenthal near Heidelberg.

The newly organized church was Presbyterian in form. Its officers were a minister, called *domine* (man of God), the elders, who had charge of church affairs, and the deacons, who collected money and took care of the sick and needy. Early in the 17th century, when The Netherlands became a sanctuary for persecuted Protestants from other countries, another officer was added to meet added responsibilities. He was a *ziekentrooster* (comforter-of-the-sick) or a *krankentrooster* (visitor-of-the-sick).

After The Netherlands became Protestant, tolerance was extended to those who remained Roman Catholic. William the Silent told his people, "You shall offer no let nor hindrance to the Roman Catholic Churches." Those who were Roman Catholics were permitted to keep to their old religion, but they were required to practice it privately and in their own homes. Their churches were closed or confiscated.

It was the Protestant Dutch Church that was established in New Netherland. In the States General's instructions to the Company is the paragraph, "They (the colonists) shall within the territory hold no·other services than that of the Reformed Religion in the manner in which they are at present conducted in this country and thus by their Christian life and conduct try to lead the Indians and other blind persons to the knowledge of God and His Word without persecuting anyone on account of his faith but leaving everyone free of conscience."

The first church service held in New Netherland was at Fort Orange in 1624, shortly after the arrival of the colonists. It was conducted by Bastiaen Jansz. Krol, comforter-of-the-sick, because no ordained minister had been sent with the settlers. The first *domine* to arrive in the Province was the Reverend Jonas Michelius, who organized the church on Manhattan Island in 1628 with Peter Minuit and his brother-in-law, Jan Huygen, as elders. By 1664 there were six ordained ministers in the Province caring for the churches on Manhattan, at Fort Orange, in Esopus, Bergen, Nieu Amstel, and the "five Dutch towns" on Long Island.

Jewish refugees from Brazil sought a home in New Amsterdam in 1654 and were permitted to remain, but they practiced their religion privately and held services only in their own houses. Three years later, the Reverend John Everardus Goetwater arrived to minister to the Lutherans, but he was not allowed to hold services even in private places; the Lutherans were required to attend the national church.

Quakers, too, were excluded until John Bowne of Vlissingen (Flushing), Long Island, permitted them to hold their "conventicles" in his house. For this he was first reprimanded by Stuyvesant,

§41. This octagonal stone building of 1680 was the second church erected in Bergen (Jersey City). Pews for women were in the center of the church and those for men around the walls. There was a high pulpit under which was a small pew with a bookrack for the use of the *voorleser*, who read the Bible and led in singing the Psalms. The church bell, installed in 1683, hung from the roof. Its services were in Dutch until well into the 19th century.

(*Old print in* Bergen & Jersey City, *E. W. Miller*)

imprisoned, and finally sent to Amsterdam for a hearing before the Company. After careful examinations, the Directors could find no fault with him and sent him back to New Amsterdam. They wrote the Director-General a letter in which they said, "The conscience of men ought to remain free and unshackled. Let everyone remain free as long as he is modest, moderate, his political conduct irreproachable, and as long as he does not offend others."

§42. The Church of St. Nicholas, "the Church in the Fort," stood at the southeast corner of Fort Amsterdam with a tablet over its door that stated in Dutch, "Year 1642 William Kieft, Director-General, hath the Commonalty caused this Temple to be built." The building was of stone, 72 feet long by 52 feet wide, and was not finished when Stuyvesant arrived in 1647. It was repaired in 1656, at which time Evert Duyckinck painted its windows with the coats of arms of New Amsterdam's influential citizens "for 2 1/2 beavers each." It suffered from fire after the surrender and was abandoned by its Dutch congregation in 1693. It is shown in *Novum Amsterodamum*, a wash drawing in sepia and colors on paper 19 1/6 inches by 5 7/8 inches, which has an inscription on its lower left margin: "In the ship Lydia by Laurens Block, son of Herman, in the year 1650." The picture was first published in 1880 by Muller of Frederick Muller & Company, The Hague, who sold it somewhat later to a Mr. Dermold.

(*New-York Historical Society*)

§43. The first church on Long Island was built in 1654-55 in Midwout, on a plot set aside for that purpose when the town was laid out in 1652. Following Stuyvesant's instructions, it was a stone cruciform building 65 feet long, 85 feet broad, and "from 12 to 14 feet under the beams." The minister's dwelling was in its rear. Its congregation was organized on February 9, 1654, and its first pastor was the Reverend Johannes Theodorus Polhemus. Standing on what is the present southwest corner of Flatbush and Church Avenues, Brooklyn, it was razed in 1698 to make way for a second church. This imaginary sketch of it is taken from the *Quarter Millenium Anniversary of the Reformed Dutch Church of Flatbush*, New York, by Cornelius L. Wells, D. D., printed in 1904.

§44. A beaten-brass weathercock was mounted on the Blockhouse Church in Beverwyck in 1656 and later transferred to the steeple of the Stone Church erected in 1715. From 1906 it showed the direction of the wind from the top of Albany's Madison Avenue Reformed Church until that building was destroyed by fire.

For centuries, cocks were used on churches as weathervanes to remind the people of Peter's three-fold denial of Christ and asseveration of love for his Master. The cock was also a symbol of Christ's resurrection.

(Albany Institute of History and Art)

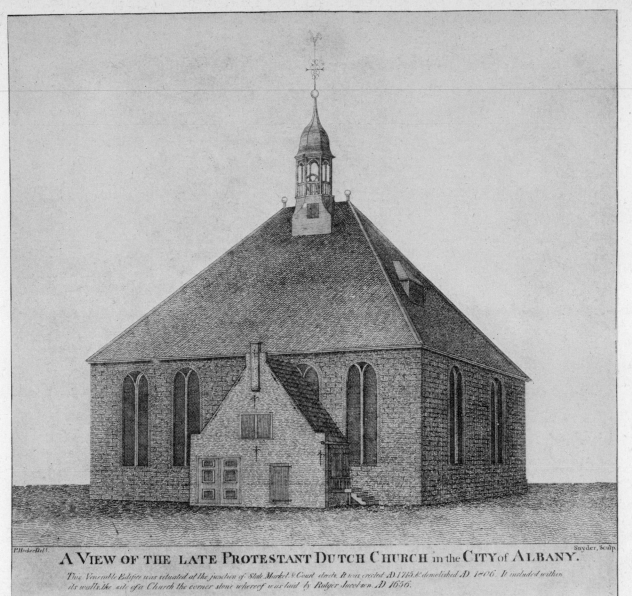

A VIEW OF THE LATE PROTESTANT DUTCH CHURCH in the CITY of ALBANY.

This Venerable Edifice was situated at the junction of State Market & Court streets. It was erected A.D. 1715 & demolished A.D. 1806. It included within its walls the site of a Church the corner stone whereof was laid by Rutger Jacobsen A.D. 1656.

§45. This picture of the Protestant Dutch Church of Albany, New York, was sketched by P. Hecker and engraved by Snyder. The edifice was built around the 1656 Blockhouse Church, interrupting services for only two weeks in October while the inner walls were being torn out. It was consecrated on November 13, 1715, and demolished in 1806. Its site is the center of Broadway and State Street in Albany.

(Albany Institute of History and Art)

§46. This is a photograph of the heraldic window made by Gerrit Duyckinck, which Jan Baptist Van Rensselaer gave to the Blockhouse Church in 1656. It was later transferred to the Church of 1715 and finally sent to a member of the Van Rensselaer family of Albany. The window, 22 1/4 by 15 1/2 inches, contained a dozen panes of glass with the Van Rensselaer arms spread over nine of them and the inscription filling the other three.

Jan Baptist Van Rensselaer, son of the Patroon Kiliaen Van Rensselaer, was born in Holland and sent by his father in 1651 to Rensselaerswyck to be its vice-director. On October 8th of that year he was made a member of its court, and on the following July 24th he assumed the duties and responsibilities of Director of the Patroonship, at an annual salary of 1,000 florin. He was succeeded by his brother Jeremias on September 24, 1658, at which time he returned to Holland. The window belongs to the Metropolitan Museum, which received it in bequest from Mrs. J. Insley Blair.

(New-York Historical Society)

§47. This section of a stained glass window made by Gerrit Duyckinck in 1657 shows a portion of the coat of arms of Commissioner Harbersen, who gave it to the Blockhouse Church. It was transferred to the 1715 Church and in 1806 sent to the donor's descendant.

Commissioner Andries Harbersen, also known as Constapel vander Vieublaes (gunner of a frigate used in Sweden), was in Rensselaerswyck as early as 1642 working as a gardener, timberman, fence-builder, and miller. By 1659 he owned a kiln for the making of bricks and tiles. In 1662 he was wounded in a tavern brawl when he stabbed and killed a man in self-defense. He died in October of that year, leaving a wife, Annetje Juriaens.

(Albany Institute of History and Art)

§48. The first edition of the Bible in Dutch was published in 1636-37 in Leiden, Holland. The copy pictured here is a very clean one and may have been the first, or among the first, off press. It is a folio Bible 16 inches tall and 5 inches thick. It was brought to New Netherland in 1647 by Petrus Stuyvesant. His father, the Reverend Balthazar Johannes Stuyvesant, was a member of the 1618-19 Synod of Dort, which appointed the committee to translate the Bible into Dutch. This Bible contains Stuyvesant family records, many of them in Dutch. It belonged to the Director-General's grandson Gerardus in 1722 and went to Gerardus's son, Petrus (1727-1805), whose daughter Cornelia, born in 1767, married Dirck Ten Broeck of Albany, New York, and died in Trenton, New Jersey, in 1825. Her husband owned the Bible until his death in 1832, after which there is no record of it until 1850, when it became the property of William Lewis B. Raymond of Summit, New Jersey. His son, William Oakley Raymond, sold it in 1933 to the late Major Edward Van Winkle of Dunellon, New Jersey.

Of the other three known copies of this edition one is in the University of Leiden Library, one is in the British Museum, and the other is owned by the New-York Historical Society.

(Exhibition of Dutch Colonial Heirlooms)

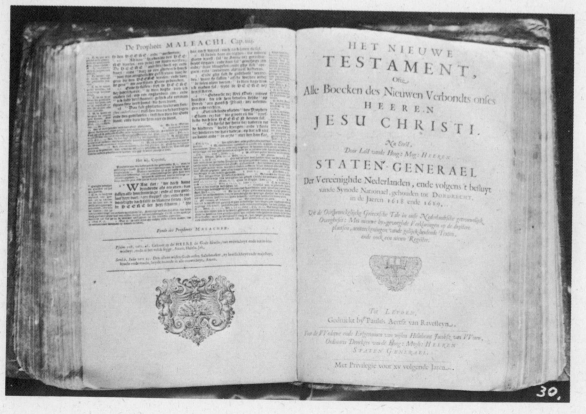

§49. A pulpit, *predickstoel* to the Dutch settlers, was built by
Francois Boon and, on August 9, 1657, installed in the Blockhouse Church of Beverwyck and Fort Orange. Boon was paid
32 florin for making the pulpit and for hanging the *kerk blockje*
(church bell), which had arrived on the *Gilt Mill* from Holland
in April, 1657.

The second church in the colony, the Blockhouse Church
was erected on a low hill west of Fort Orange to replace the
original church. Its cornerstone was laid on June 2, 1656. It
was a fortified building which could be used as a place of
safety in case of Indian attacks.

(First Church of Albany, New York)

§50. This silver beaker, with the letters H B M on the bottom,
was made in Holland in 1638 and sent at an early, but unknown, date to New Amsterdam, possibly for use in the
Church of St. Nicholas. It is engraved with strapwork and
with figures symbolizing Fortitude, Strength, and Wisdom.
*(Collegiate Reformed Protestant Dutch Church of the City
of New York)*

§51. This pair of silver beakers, made by Gerritt Onkelbag (1670-1732), was given to the Church of Flatbush, Long Island, and was exhibited during the church's tercentenary celebrations in 1954. The beakers are now on loan at the Brooklyn Museum.

(Brooklyn Museum)

§52. This hatchment was painted in the first half of the 18th century by an anonymous artist on canvas 25 3/4 inches square. It has a black background, tan draperies and scrolls, and a white shield and bull's head. The initials G. V. S. in its design no doubt stood for Goosen or Gerrit van Schaik, both of Albany, New York.

A hatchment was a funeral emblem that was hung in houses and churches and carried in funeral processions. Based on heraldic designs, it was usually owned by a family of wealth and distinction.

(Albany Institute of History and Art)

§53. This silver beaker is one of a pair given on October 3, 1684, to the Brooklyn Church by Maria Baddia, who joined the church on September 27, 1662, when she is mentioned in its records as "Maria Baddia, nee Bennett, nee Thomas, wife of Paulus Vander Beeck." The beaker is 7 1/4 inches high. Its lip is 3 1/4 inches in diameter, and its base, 3 inches. Helen Burr Smith attributes the maker's mark on its bottom to Juriaen Blanck, Jr., who was working as a silversmith in New York as early as 1666, and who was the husband of Hester Vander Beeck.

(Reformed Protestant Dutch Church of Brooklyn, New York)

§54. A number of the original Dutch churches were copies of, or similar to, the earliest Protestant churches of The Netherlands, the first of which was erected in 1595 at Willemstadt, Holland.

The New Utrecht, Long Island, Church was built about 1700 on a lot (presently 84th Street between 16th and 17th Avenues, Brooklyn) laid out for a church and cemetery in 1657 by Jacques Cortelyou, founder of the town. Until its erection, the members of its congregation, organized in 1677, attended services in either the Brooklyn or the Flatbush Church.

(Long Island Historical Society)

§55. The Bushwick, Long Island, Church was probably erected between 1708, the date on its Communion Beaker, and 1711, when a bill for its bell dated 1706 and sent from Holland was receipted. The church stood on *Het Dorp*, later Bushwick Common and now the vicinity of Conselyea and Humboldt Streets, Brooklyn. Since it originally contained no pews, its members supplied their own seats. It was demolished in 1827. As it was one of Long Island's Collegiate Churches, its first ministers were the Reverend Bernardus Freeman and the Reverend Vicnetius Antonides who took turns in conducting its services. This picture was painted by C. T. Meeker for a lithograph published by G. Hayward & Company in 1868.

§56. The pewter beaker that was used in the Bushwick Church has the touchmark of a rose on its bottom and the date 1708 near its top between two rows of wriggle work, together with the suggestion in Dutch, "Eat what is good, drink what is pure, speak what is true."

(Long Island Historical Society)

In this Vault lies buried
PETRUS STUYVESANT,
late Captain General and Governor in Chief, of Amsterdam
in New-Netherland now called New-York
and the Dutch West-India Islands, died in A.D. 167½
aged 80 years.

171

§57. The stone that marks the Stuyvesant burial vault is in
the east wall of the Protestant Episcopal Church of St.
Marks- in-the-Bowery, Second Avenue and 10th Street,
New York City. The church is on the site of the chapel built
by Stuyvesant in 1662 on his bowery, northeast of his
house. The vault was under the chapel which his wife, who
died in 1687, deeded to the Dutch Reformed Church of New
York. Since there was no money left for maintenance, the
chapel fell into decay and was a ruin in 1793, when the
Director-General's great-grandson, Petrus Stuyvesant, an
Episcopalian, gave it to the Trinity Church Corporation,
with $1,800 and the ground, 150 feet by 190 feet, on which
it stood. The corporation removed the ruins and in 1796
erected the present church with the Stuyvesant vault under
it. The vault was sealed in 1953 after the interment of
August Van Cortlandt Stuyvesant, the last of the American
family to bear his illustrious surname.

§58. This silver beaker was made by Henricus Boelen (1697-
1755). It has a border of repeated crosses at the base, its
sides flare gradually to a plain rim at the top. It is engraved
with three medallions, each enclosing a woman and an
inscription in Latin. The medallions are connected and
surrounded by graceful leaf and floral sprays and strapwork.
The beaker belongs to the Dutch Church of Flatlands, Long
Island, and is on loan at the Brooklyn Museum.

(Brooklyn Museum)

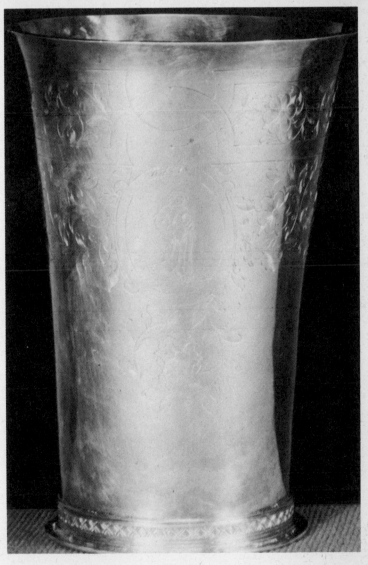

§59. This "Psalm Book for Four Voices," printed in Holland, contains the ritual of the Protestant Reformed Dutch Church and the Psalms set to music and arranged so that four singers can use the book, provided they stand in couples and face each other. In 1780 it belonged to Jan Ver Kerk Van Nuyse (born in 1751), who was *voorsanger* (leader of the singing) in the New Utrecht, Long Island, Church. In 1940 the psaltery was in the hands of his descendant, the late Miss Maude E. Voris of Brooklyn, New York.

§60. Many women who regularly attended the Dutch church services in New Netherland, and later in New York and New Jersey, owned a small New Testament printed in Holland. With the Apocalypse and the Psalms, which were often set to music, it was bound in leather and adorned with silver or brass corners, clasp, and chain. This, with A. L. engraved on the inner side of the silver clasp, belonged to Abigail Lefferts Lloyd (1759-1847) of Flatbush. In 1950, it was in the possession of Mrs. Herman Hagedorn of Brooklyn, Abigail Lloyd's great-great-great-great-granddaughter.

CHAPTER FOUR
New Netherland Domestic Architecture

Plates 61-81

§61. The building that became New Amsterdam's *Stadt Huys* was built in 1641 at the foot of a low hill on the Strand (Pearl Street east of Broad Street, New York City). It was 42 feet broad by 52 feet deep and consisted of a basement, two stories, two lofts above the top story, and a kitchen at the rear. On January 1, 1642, it was leased for a tavern to Philip Gerritsen from Haarlem for six years at an annual rental of 300 guilders. The following year it was filled with refugees fleeing from Indian attacks caused by Kieft's unjust treatment of the redmen. It was the meeting place for the Company's officials and the better class of citizens, though sometimes the meetings were interrupted by such occurrences as a brawl in which a man "had a piece of his ear cut off by a cutlass." In 1653 the tavern was closed and the building became the City Hall. The cupola and dormer windows were then added and its entrance, which had faced the Fort, was changed to face the East River. Gerrit Duyckinck painted the city's arms on a window in its Council Chamber, and this "was pointed to with pride for Forty years." The picture is of a lithograph made by G. Hayward & Company from a sketch made by Danckers for his Journal.

(New-York Historical Society)

New Netherland Domestic Architecture

CORNELIS VAN TIENHOVEN, while secretary of New Netherland, issued a pamphlet in 1650 entitled *Information Relative to Taking Land in New Netherland*. In it he said that the immigrants on their arrival dug pits in the earth, floored and lined them with wood, and "erected roofs with sods or bark."

In 1626, the year in which New Amsterdam was laid out, the settlers were living in thirty bark-covered houses on Manhattan Island. But, according to the Reverend Michelius, who wrote to his colleagues in Holland, two years later "houses were being built to replace these hovels in which they (the settlers) huddled rather than dwelt."

By July 9, 1638, there was a house standing on the bowery of Achterveldt at Nieu Amersfoort, Long Island, which belonged to Wolphert Gerritsen Van Cowenhoven and was described as follows:

" . . . .One house surrounded by long, round palisades; the house 26 feet long, 22 feet wide, and 40 feet deep with a roof covered above and all around with planks, two garrets, one above the other, and a small chamber on the side with an outlet on the side."

At the time of the surrender, dwellings in the Province were substantial, comfortable and even handsome. The larger houses of Beverwyck and New Amsterdam were usually of stone or brick with three or four stories above the cellar. Their blue or red pantile roofs were steeply pitched. Under the stepped gable which faced the road, was a substantial raised doorstep (*stoep*) for the main entrance. Farmhouses generally were wooden-frame structures although occasionally one might be built of masonry. Most of these had one story with a low loft above and a lean-to built against one wall, used as a milkroom. The houses were built close to the ground and their roofs sloped in a broad, gentle curve to project beyond the walls. For the most part the first type was prevalent in upper New York State, and the latter in southern New York, western Long Island, and New Jersey. Frame houses were often covered with shingles instead of clapboards, and as the Dutch were the first colonists to use shingles for that purpose, houses so covered are sometimes said "to be in the Dutch fashion."

It was a practice on Long Island, whenever feasible, to face the house to the south so that its interior would have as much sun as possible on the short winter days.

Often the north side of the roof fell to within four or five feet of the ground. With neither door nor window in the north wall, manure was piled against it in the autumn and covered with salt hay that was held in place by planks. In the spring the thrifty Dutch farmers spread this hay, entirely rotted, on their gardens for fertilizer.

Throughout the Province roofs were often thatched. This continued until Stuyvesant and his council banned thatch as a fire hazard. Chimneys were always built within the walls, only their broad upper parts visible on the outside of a building. They were at the ends of frame structures, in which case the brick or stone back of the fireplace formed a rectangle on the outer side of the wall.

Windows varied. For the most part they were casements divided into transoms, the lower sections opening inward. Shed dormers, often called Dutch dormers, lighted chambers under the roof. Occasionally, a circular window was used, and frequently a bull's-eye, made of molten glass, was set in the entrance door to give light to a dark interior. Leaden window frames were imported from Holland as were window panes, although glass was being made in New Amsterdam by the 1650's.

§62. "Neefus Homestead, Cow Lane, Flatbush," is the title of this sketch by A. Droste. Cow Lane, later East Broadway, was the original name of Church Avenue east of Flatbush Avenue in Brooklyn. On Dr. Strong's map of Flatbush, 1842, the property at the southeast corner of the two streets belonged to Michael Neefus. Mrs. Vanderbilt, in her *History of Flatbush*, wrote that the house had been built in Flatbush's earliest days (it was settled in 1652) by a member of the Waldron family and had descended through the Fish and Strycker families to Neefus. It was partly torn down in 1881, and some of its timbers were used in a store built on its site.

(*Long Island Historical Society*)

§63. The Vander Heyden mansion stood on the west side of North Pearl Street, south of Maiden Lane, in Albany, until it was torn down in 1833, at which time Washington Irving acquired its weathervane for his "Sunnyside." Built in 1725 for Johannes Beekman, the house was 50 feet broad by 20 feet deep. It had a wide central hall on its main floor with three rooms on each side of it. The block and tackle attached to a beam at the top of each gable was useful in lifting heavy articles into the upper rooms. The house was sold to Jacobus Vander Heyden in 1778. It was used by Washington Irving in his story of Bracebridge Hall as the home of Antony van der Heyden.

(*Albany Institute of History and Art*)

Imported panes were always 12 inches by 8 inches, and often had to be cut to fit the frames into which they were set. Such was the case mentioned in a New Amsterdam court record on January 12, 1654, when Hendrick Hendricksen complained that Claes Croon "sometime back took with him a pane of glass out of his house to make them (*sic*) somewhat smaller so as to fit, which up to the present date he has not returned, so that he suffered great inconvenience from this wintery weather."

Shutters to the lower transoms were hinged outside the windows so as to swing outward. Those of upper transoms were hinged at top inside the windows and could be hooked above them against the ceilings. Shutters generally were made of a piece of solid wood, framed by rails and styles that met at angles. Entrance doors were constructed similarly and divided horizontally, permitting the upper part to be opened while the lower part remained closed.

A beam often extended from an aperture in the loft of a house, as can still be seen in old buildings in Amsterdam and Delft. To it was attached a block and tackle by means of which heavy articles could be lifted into the upper stories. Sometimes, the date of a building's erection was shown in brass or iron figures at least a foot long, fastened to the exterior masonry.

§64. This "View of Houses in the City of Albany" was shown in the Columbia Magazine for December, 1789.

(*Albany Institute of History and Art*)

A View of Houſes *in the* CITY *of* ALBANY.

§65. The Widow Sturdevant's house, as it was called, was built in Beverwyck in the mid 17th century for the colony's baker on Pearl Street, five
doors north of Maiden Lane. It was altered about 1805 when its entrance
and front door were changed. It is thought to have been demolished in the
1870's.

(*Albany Institute of History and Art*)

§66. This, Stuyvesant's Bowery Mansion, may have been the building erected by the Company's carpenters in 1633 for Wouter Van Twiller on Bowery No. 1. On March 12, 1661, the Amsterdam Directors authorized the sale of the Bowery "with its dwelling house, barns, woods, and six cows, 2 horses and 2 young Negroes" for 6,400 guilders to Jan Jansz. Damen, agent for Petrus Stuyvesant. Nicholas William Stuyvesant inherited the bulk of his father's estate but did not move into the mansion until after his mother's death. His son Gerardus was living in it in July, 1758, when it was visited by du Simitiere, who wrote that the house was a short mile from town, built in the Dutch style, and stood on the right hand side of the lane leading from the main road called the Bowery Road. (Its site is on the east side of Third Avenue between 10th and 11th Streets, New York City.) He also noticed that the house contained many small panes of painted glass that had formerly been in its chapel.

Nicholas Stuyvesant was occupying the house when it caught fire at two a.m. on October 14, 1778, and burned to the ground. Hessian officers must have had a billet there at the time, for the Hessian Colonel Munckhausen set a guard to watch the possessions that had been saved and left the guard to the direction of the family when he departed later in the morning.

(*Long Island Historical Society*)

§67. Stuyvesant's Great House stood on the south side of Pearl Street near the foot of Whitehall Street in New York City. It was built before February 14, 1648, when the New Netherland Council deeded the property to the Director-General. It was sold after his death and was later owned by Governor Thomas Dongan, who named it White Hall.

(*Long Island Historical Society*)

§68. This photograph is of a sketch made on paper 72 inches by 92 inches by George T. Plowman. On its back is written, "The Wyckoff Homestead, Flatlands Neck, Carnarsie Lane near Kings Highway, Brooklyn, N. Y. 1922." The house was built by the Company's carpenters about 1639 on Long Island property that Wouter Van Twiller bought from the Indians in July, 1636. It was confiscated by the Company on his recall to Holland and was occupied by Pieter Claesen, superintendent of "the Bowery and Cattle" of Director-General Stuyvesant in 1655. The property was deeded to the Town of Flatlands after the surrender and is shown on its map of 1719 as "onthevided (*sic*) land laid out for Claes Wyckoff." (Pieter Claesen's son)

The house is standing on a triangle of land at Carnarsie Lane, Clarendon Road, and Ralph Avenue, Brooklyn. The Wyckoff House Foundation was chartered in 1960 for the purpose of saving it and making it into a historic shrine as the oldest house on Long Island.

(*Courtesy of Mr. Daniel Streeter*)

§69. This house, one of the oldest in Delaware, was erected by a Dutch settler in 1662 across from the Common of Nieu Amstel. It still stands on its original site, now 32 East Third Street, New Castle, Delaware, carefully restored, authentically furnished, and open to the public. This sketch of the old house was made by J. B. Moll, Jr., of Oxford, Maryland.

§70. This stone house, minus the wing, was built after 1643, when Indians burned all Gowanus houses, and before 1666, when it is shown on a Gowanus map as being on a large plot of ground bordering on New York Bay, across which is written, "said to be sold to Simon Arison."

Simon Aesen Ter Heart (De Hart) arrived at New Amsterdam, married Geertje Cornelissen, and bought his farm in 1664. His granddaughter Gertie, wife of Simon Bergen, inherited his house. In the autumn of 1679, he was visited by the Labadists, who noted in their Journal:

"Symon took us into his house and entertained us exceedingly well. We found a good fire half-way up the chimney of clear oak and hickory which they make not the least scruple of burning profusely. We let it penetrate us thoroughly. There had already been thrown upon it to be roasted a pail-full of Gowanus oysters, which are the best in the country, some not less than a foot long. We had for supper a roasted haunch of venison, bought of the Indians for 3 1/2 guilders in seawan, tender, good and quite fat, with slightly spicy flavor; wild turkey, also fat and of good flavor and wild duck whose meat was rather dry."

On another visit, they found Jacques Cortelyou, former Surveyor-General of New Netherland at Simon's, treating his horse for the staggers. That night, the Indians whom Geertje had allowed to build huts on the beach "got lustily drunk, ranting, raving, striking, jumping, fisting each other, and foaming at the mouth like raving wild beasts. Those who were sober took their wives and children into Symon's house for safety."

(*Long Island Historical Society*)

§71. A house with a typically Flemish roof stood until the mid-1920's in the Flatlands section of Brooklyn on what was originally called Vriesen's Hoek, later Flatlands Neck. It was west of Kings Highway and in the vicinity of Avenue D. It was the home of Willem Gerritsen Van Cowenhoven after his marriage to Jannetje Montfoort, his second wife, in February, 1665.

As in all Dutch farmhouses of New Netherland, only the upper portion of its chimney is visible; the large rectangle of brick (or stone) is the back of its fireplace.

§72. A postcard sold in the early 20th century by F. A. Lippold, Flatbush Avenue, Brooklyn. According to tradition, the house pictured above is the one mentioned by Danckers in his *Journal*

of a Voyage to New York in 1679-80, on October 8, 1674:

"Elbert (Elbert Elbertse Stoothoff) and his wife bade us welcome. They took us around their orchards to look at them. His house was constantly filled with a multitude of Godless people, for Elbert, being the principal man in the place, was their captain, and having many children of his own, there was a constant concourse in his house."

Danckers added that Elbert kept store in his house where he sold dry goods, groceries, hardware, liquor, grains, skins, oil, whalebone, etc., and where "farmers of The Bay (Flatlands) congregated on stormy days." (His account books are now in the possession of the Colonial Daughters of the Seventeenth Century.)

After his former dwelling burned in 1674, Elbert built on Van Cowenhoven property which he acquired when he married Altje Cool, widow of Gerrit Wolphertsen Van Cowenhoven, in August, 1645, by promising to pay Gerrit's debts and educate his four children, one of whom was "weak in the legs." The house stood until 1849 on the east side of Flatbush Avenue, a short distance north of Kings Highway (now part of Brooklyn). It was replaced by J. H. Hendricksen's General Store which was still doing business in the early 1920's.

§73. A drawing, signed by Lossing-Barritt and shown in Lossing's *Field Book of the Revolution*, is of one of the first three houses erected in Nieu Utrecht, Long Island. It was built in 1657 by the carpenter Jacob Hellakers, also called Jacob Swartz, for Nicasius De Sille, Schout-Fiscal of New Netherland and a founder of Nieu Utrecht as well as its first town clerk. (He divorced his second wife on grounds of incompatibility.) Surrounded by a stout palisade, the house stood on the present 18th Avenue near 84th Street, Brooklyn. Its roof was covered with red pantiles, a few of which are now owned by the Long Island Historical Society. The house was demolished in 1850.

Before publishing his book, Lossing asked Miss Catharine Lott of New Utrecht to make a sketch of De Sille's house for him, and this picture may have been copied from hers.

(*Long Island Historical Society*)

§74. The Demarest farmhouse, formerly on the east bank of the Hackensack River, now stands in the grounds of the Bergen County Historical Society at North Hackensack, New Jersey.

David Des Marest, a Huguenot born in 1620 in Beauchamp, Picardy, arrived on the *Bonte Koe* (Spotted Cow) at New Amsterdam in April, 1663, with his wife Marie Sohiere, and their sons, David and Jean. After living with the French colonists on Staten Island and in Harlem, he obtained a grant of 5,000 acres on the Hackensack River, then called the Herring, and there built his stone and timber, two-room house in 1678. It has an entrance door leading into each of its rooms, as did many of the small Dutch houses.

(*Bergen County Historical Society*)

§75. This dwelling in New Paltz, New York, has the steeply pitched roof so typical of the houses of Holland. Like other dwellings in the village and its first church, erected in 1683, its walls are of stone and its gables under the eaves of wood. Originally, there was no window in its upper story, but there was a transom containing ten panes of glass over its Dutch entrance door and, to the left of the door, a broad shuttered window of thirty glasses, each 7 inches by 9 inches.

The house was built by Louis Bevier, the leader of the Huguenots who settled New Paltz in the spring of 1678. He was born in Lille in 1648 and escaped from France and the soldiers of Louis XIV to the Palatinate. In 1673 he married Maria Le Blanc, also from Lille, and in 1675 he arrived with his wife in New York. At his death in 1720, the house went to his son Samuel. In 1765, it was bought by Josiah Eltinge, "the richest man in the town," whose descendants are still living in it.

(Photograph by Leo C. Spies)

§76. In February, 1699, the Common Council of New York undertook to improve conditions at the ferry landing in Brooklyn. At a cost of 435 pounds they erected a ferry house, with a front of 24 feet and a depth of 40 feet, and "containing five fireplaces with jambs." It was to be used for both a ferry house and a tavern. On December 29, 1700, the City Corporation leased it to Dirk Benson for seven years at an annual rental of 130 pounds, describing it as "a new brick house, barns and a pen (for cattle) hereunto pertaining."

The above engraving of the ferry house was published by Thomas Blackwell, London, in 1746. It was probably copied from the Burger View of New York, made in 1716-18 and issued in 1719-21.

§77. Iron figures more than a foot long, 1699, dated the erection of this stone and brick farmhouse that was known until its demolition in the 1870's as the "Vechte-Cortelyou House" and the "Old Stone House at Gowanus." It was built by Klaes Arents Vechte, who arrived at New Amsterdam from the Province of Drenthe on the *Bonte Koe* (Spotted Cow) with his wife and three sons in April, 1660. Years later he obtained the grant of land in the Gowanus section of Brooklyn on which he built his house. Around it was fought the principal engagement of the Battle of Long Island on August 27, 1776. At the turn of the century it became the property of the Cortelyou family, which owned it in 1846, when Louis Gruber painted this picture of it.

§78. The Vanderveer barn stood on the east side of Flatbush Avenue near Avenue D in Brooklyn until it was demolished in 1911. It was the property of the descendants of Cornelis Jansz. van der Veer (from the ferry), who arrived in New Netherland from Alkmaar in North Holland in 1659. Two years later he married Tryntje Gillis Mandeville and obtained a grant of land in the southern part, the *Rustenberg* (resting place), of Midwout (Flatbush) and there established his home, building a small house and, maybe, this barn. It was a frame building covered with shingles almost two feet long. A number of these are now owned by the Long Island Historical Society.

(*Long Island Historical Society*)

§79 & 80. Johannis Schenck, a farmer living in the "disputed" land between Bushwick and Newtown, Long Island, built a small house on the west end of his property in about 1721 for his son Peter, who was married prior to August 29th of that year. It was a shingled frame house that consisted of one room with a loft above it. The house faces the south, and the north slope of its roof falls to within a few feet of the ground. Sixty-five years after its erection, Nicholas Wyckoff used it as the kitchen wing of the dwelling he built, now 1325 Flushing Avenue, Brooklyn. The side windows were probably added at that time.

The other picture shows the *stoep* (stoop) at the entrance of the Peter Schenck house, although, possibly, not the original. The 18th-century shingles have been replaced by clapboards; the shutters are from the 19th century, while the screen door is modern.

(Courtesy of Miss Edna Huntington)

§81. The Dutch door shown here is on a house, 1669 East 22nd Street, Brooklyn, that is the home of the Reverend and Mrs. Frank Curtis Williams. It was built in 1766 by Abraham and Hendrick Wyckoff on their Gravesend, Long Island, farm, which was sold in 1834 to Cornelis W. Bennett. The house originally faced south, but it was turned in the early days of the 20th century to face the west. At that time the dormers, porch, and shutters at the front door were added.

Mrs. Williams, who was born in the house, is Brooklyn's poet, Gertrude Ryder Bennett.

CHAPTER FIVE
Inside New Netherland Homes

Plates 82-101

Inside New Netherland Homes

WRITING of the Dutch houses in her *Journal of a Trip to New York* in 1704, Madam Knight, a Boston lady, had this to say: "The insides of them is neat to admiration, for only the walls are plastered, and the Soners and gist are planed and kept very white, and scour'd as so is all the partitions made of bords. . . . The fireplaces have no Jambs (as ours have). But the backs are flush with the Walls, and the Hearth is of Tyles, and is as far out in the Room at the ends as before the fire, which is generally five foot in the Low'r rooms, and the piece over where the Mantel tree should be is made as ours with Joyners work, and I suppose is fastened with iron rods inside."

Hearths were not always of tiles; some were of stone or brick. Instead of in recessed fireplaces, fires were laid on the hearth against the wall. A pendant hood extended far over the hearth and allowed smoke to escape up its chimney. Usually a shelf was built on the three extending edges of the hood, and on this were displayed the family treasures; maybe only a pewter tankard or plate in the more simple homes, but in the houses of prosperous colonists there might be tankards or porringers of silver, and plates of Dutch or Oriental china. A *schoorsteen valletje* (fireplace valance) hung from the bottom of the shelf; checked linen in the kitchens, but richer materials in the parlors, such as printed calico, East India cotton goods, serge trimmed with fringe, silk damask, even "flowered crimson gauze." The valance often matched the window draperies and the bed hangings if a bed were in the room. Industrious housewives who lived in Long Island farmhouses changed their checked linen valances every Saturday morning, removing the used one and replacing it with one freshly washed and ironed.

The lower parts of the inner walls were sometimes wainscoted or covered with tiles; the upper walls were plastered with a clay mixed with chopped hay and then whitewashed.

Before English influence was felt, inner doors were like the outside shutters, of a plank of wood framed, the rails cutting across the stiles at right angles. Such a door may be seen in the Jean Hasbrouck house, New Paltz, New York, which is the property of the Huguenot Association and open to the public.

§82. This room in the Museum of the City of New York was arranged by Miss V. Isabelle Miller, Curator of the Costume, Furniture, and Silver Collections. It could have been the living room in the home of a prosperous New York Dutch family in the late 17th century. The window, door, and door casement came from a late 17th-century Hudson Valley house, and the furnishings are authentic. The clothes are copied from Dutch paintings of the period, as are the collar and chain on the neck of the squirrel.

(Museum of the City of New York)

Floors were uncarpeted. They were often sanded except in bedrooms. On Long Island, where no house was a great distance from a beach, the sand was changed weekly. While still damp, it was placed in small mounds in a room and then swept with a broom into geometric designs by a beauty-loving housewife or her Negro slave. And woe betide the child or man who put foot on that floor before the sand had dried!

A typical stepped-gable house, like those in Beverwyck, Fort Orange, and New Amsterdam, consisted of a cellar, sometimes with a cellar-kitchen, a front and back room on the main floor, chambers on the second story, a cock loft above them, and a garret under the eaves. The front room on the main floor was frequently used for a store or office.

Farmhouses varied as much in their floor plans as they did in their exterior appearance. But they almost always had an extension at one end which had an earthen floor and was used for a milk room. A house might contain but one principal room with a smaller room, *kamertje*, behind it and a loft above. Or again it might have two adjoining front rooms, each with its own entrance door, and a loft over both. More important dwellings had a central hall one or two rooms deep, a loft above and, maybe, a second loft above that. Often the portion of a loft or garret around the chimney was partitioned off; this small room served as a storage place for meats that had been smoked in an out building used only for the purpose of smoking food.

The Dutch used a number of lighting fixtures: brass and copper chandeliers, silver and brass candlesticks, the *izer knaap*, which was a standing iron receptacle for candles often decorated with a brass finial, and wooden stands in which rushes were clipped to their arms.

The bed was generally an integral part of a room and built into its walls like an alcove; this was called a *slaap banck*. Those who could afford to do so sometimes imported a movable, paneled, closet-like bed from Holland. (Stuyvesant is said to have owned such a bed.) And as a makeshift sleeping accommodation there was always the "kermis bed," nothing more or less than a ticking filled with hay, straw, or corn husks, and laid on the floor.

Many of the houses, even the more simple ones, were well and comfortably furnished, similarly to those shown in the genre paintings of Jan Steen, Pieter de Hooch, Vermeer and other 17th-century Dutch artists. A few had pictured "storied glasses" in

§83. This "storied" pane of 17th-century glass illustrates the Dutch proverb, "Two fools with their silly pranks never sat long on the same donkey." One of three panes in sepia, it may have been made by Evert or Gerrit Duyckinck for the house of some wealthy New Amsterdam burgher and later transferred to the Eighth Street house in New York from which it was rescued. It is now in Dr. Haagensen's country home at Sneeden's Landing on the Hudson. (*Courtesy of Dr. Cushman Haagensen*)

their windows. A portrait or two, brought from the homeland or maybe painted locally, hung on the walls together with a small mirror or Friesland clock. "Turkey carpets" covered small tables, and draperies were at the windows. Some of the furniture was brought in from Holland, but the remainder was made by New Netherland carpenters.

One of the wealthiest men of the Dutch period, Cornelis Van Steenwyck, at the time of his death, had in the parlor of his house on Pearl Street, in New York, "a marble table, a wooden table, 7 Russian leather chairs, a crumb-cloth (which is said to be a carpet used under the dining table), a foot bench, curtains, 3 cushions and a clock."

In the back, or family room were "12 Russian leather chairs, 2 velvet chairs with silver lace, a cupboard, a round table, a square table, a bedstead with 2 beds, 10 pieces of china, 5 alabaster images, tapestry work for 12 cushions, flowered tabby chimney cloth (a fireplace valance) and flowered tabby window curtains, a dressing box, table linen."

§84. This ash and beech chair with rush seat and cane back was made between 1680 and 1700. It belonged to Dr. Hans Kiersted, who arrived at New Amsterdam in 1633 as the Company's chirugeon. He married Sarah Roeloffs, daughter of Annetje Jans and stepdaughter of *Domine* Bogardus. He owned a farm on Bowery Lane, about one-and-a-half miles north of the city, but made his home on the site now the northeast corner of Pearl and Whitehall Streets, New York City. His descendant, Mrs. Leonard Cox of New York, gave the chair in 1954 to the Museum of the City of New York.

(Museum of the City of New York)

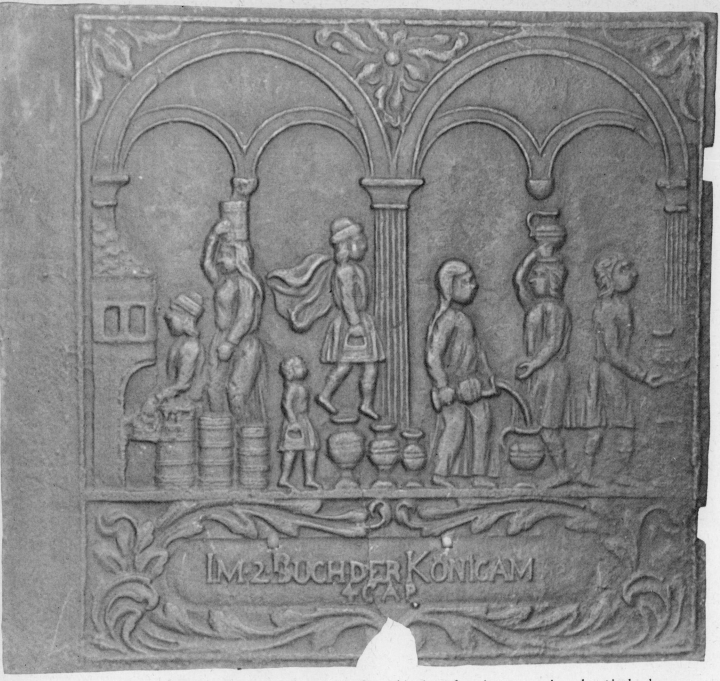

§85. This piece of cast iron, approximately 36 inches by 30 inches, may have been the side of a stove, the kind used in the 18th century by the Palatines and other natives of the Rhine Valley. It has on it a design representing the filling of the widows' oil pots, with the inscription below: *Im 2 Buch der Kongam 4 Cap.*

It was taken by Abraham van Leuren (originally Keulen), Jr., from his boyhood home in Kingston, New York, to Rhinebeck, New York, after his marriage to Evatje Du Mont on October 28, 1777. His son Garret installed it as a fireback in 1800 in his new house on Spring Brook Farm, Rhinebeck. When that was being razed, Garret's granddaughter, Helen Reed Delaporte (Mrs. Theodore) rescued the fireback, which is now in the Rhinebeck home of Mrs. Anna (Mitchell) Hill, descendant of Captain Mattys Matthysen van Keuelen, patentee of Esopus.

(*Mrs. Harry H. Hill*)

§86. The ruffle hanging from the edge of the mantel in the above picture was called a *schoorsteen valletje* by the Dutch settlers. The jambless fireplace is in the oldest part of the Billou-Stillwell-Perine House, 1476 Richmond Avenue, Dongan Hills, Staten Island, New York. It was built by Pierre Billou, a Huguenot who arrived in New Amsterdam in 1661 and was given a grant of land on Staten Island on which to settle. His fireplace was later hidden by two fireplaces with jambs and was not discovered until the 1940's, when it was restored to what may have been its original appearance.

(Staten Island Historical Society)

§87. The jambless fireplace in Washington's Headquarters, Washington and Liberty Streets, Newburgh, New York, was built in 1750 by Jonathan Hasbrouck. It has a height of 8 feet 4 inches, an opening of 8 feet by 3 feet 4 inches, and a hearth 8 feet 1 inch by 4 feet 8 inches wide.

(Washington's Headquarters, Newburgh, New York)

Boutrelle
New York

§88. This cradle was used for generations by babies of the Gravesend, Long Island, family descended from Bernardus Ryder (1688-1769). Although locally made, it is similar to one owned by the descendants of Willem Gerretsen Cowenhoven, a patentee of Flatlands, Long Island, in 1677. The late Major Van Winkel of Dunellon, New Jersey, claimed that it was exactly like one owned by his ancestor, Jacob Walich Van Winkel, who arrived from Hoorn, North Holland, in 1624. He lived for a time on the Company's Bowery No. 5 and was given a grant of land in 1654 near Communipaw in Pavonia, now part of New Jersey.

§89. Stuyvesant is said to have owned a panelled bedstead brought from Holland. It was probably similar to the Dutch bed imported from Amsterdam in the early 20th century by the Colonial Dames of the State of New York and placed by them in the Van Cortlandt Mansion, Van Cortlandt Park, City of New York.

(*National Society of Colonial Dames, State of New York*)

§90 (OPPOSITE). A recessed bed in the Canarsie, Long Island, house that was built by Nicklaes Schenck in 1758. It is now in the Brooklyn Museum.

(*Brooklyn Museum*)

§91. This gateleg table, in the style of William and Mary, was made by an unknown Hudson Valley carpenter at the end of the 17th or beginning of the 18th century for the Manor House of the Van Cortlandt family at Croton-on-the-Hudson. It still stands in the dining room of the house, which is now a museum open to the public. Made of mahogany with iron butterfly hinges, the table has a height of 27 3/4 inches. Its top, when spread out, measures 58 inches by 72 1/4 inches.

(Sleepy Hollow Restoration)

§92. This small walnut table has its top decorated with designs in ash and rosewood, its drawer lined with tulip poplar. Originally it belonged to Aert Middagh (1707-1777), whose descendant, Lea S. Luquer, lent it for exhibition in the Museum of the City of New York. Aert Middagh was a grandson of the Aert Middagh who came to New Netherland in 1661, for the second time, arriving on the *Beaver*. He married Breckje Hansen Bergen and established his farm on Iphetonga (Brooklyn Heights). In 1817, Middagh Street in Brooklyn was cut through his farm.

(Museum of the City of New York)

§93. This walnut chair, having a leather back and seat that are held in place by brass-headed nails, belonged to Sarah Rapalje, who is believed to be the first girl of European parents born in New Netherland. The chair was made in New Netherland after 1639, the date of her first marriage, and before 1685, about the time of her death. Her daughter Annetje Bogart, wife of Joris Brinckerhoff, evidently inherited it, for it was owned by her descendant, the late Mrs. Henry Clapp (Emily Brinckerhoff) of Pleasantville, New York, until it became the property of the Museum of the City of New York.

(Museum of the City of New York)

§94. This armchair of oak with matted seat was made between 1680 and 1700 and belonged to the Riker family of Newtown, Long Island. Probably Abraham, born in New Amsterdam in 1655, was its first owner. He married Grietje Gerrits van Buytenhuysen and lived with his family on his farm at the Poor Bowery, Newtown. He had inherited this from his father, together with an island in the East River that was originally called Hewlett's, and now Riker's. *(Museum of the City of New York)*

§95. This pine *kas*, put together with wooden pins, is of Long Island manufacture and was probably made early in the 18th century. It stood for generations in a Bergen farmhouse on Kings Highway (near 38th Street), Flatlands. In the first quarter of the 20th century, it was given to the Kings County Historical Society by Theodore Bergen, eldest son of Jeremiah Bergen of Gowanus, who married Jane Ann, daughter of Jeromus Lott of Flatlands and went to her home town to live. It is now owned by the Long Island Historical Society, as part of its Kings County Historical Society collection.

(*Long Island Historical Society*)

§96. The handsome *kas* that is in the Van Cortlandt Mansion, Van Cortlandt Park, New York, was imported from Holland by Doctor Samuel Staats as part of the wedding outfit of his daughter, Catharine, who married Stephen Van Cortlandt in 1713. It is now owned by their descendant, Mrs. Van Rensselaer Wittmann of New York.

(*Museum of the City of New York*)

§97. The *kas* pictured here was presented to the Brooklyn Museum by Miss Mary Van Kleek of Brooklyn in memory of her brother, Dr. Charles Van Kleek. It was made in Holland about 1650 and brought to New Netherland by Barnet Baltus, who settled in Midwout (Flatbush) where his children were also baptized under the name of Baltus. He most probably assumed the surname of Van Kleeck shortly after the surrender, when men of Dutch extraction were ordered by the English to have a surname. *(Brooklyn Museum)*

§98. This Bible box, shown in Wallace Nutting's *Furniture Treasury*, is covered with Friesland carving and has handwrought iron butterfly hinges fastened by handmade iron nails. It was made in America, probably in New York, between 1675 and 1700.

(Brooklyn Museum)

§99. This sea chest was brought to New Amsterdam by *Domine* Bogardus. It is 36 inches long, 24 inches wide, and 22 inches deep, has a hand-wrought brass escutcheon, handmade iron bails and handles, and a lock of early 17th-century design. Authorities on antiques disagree on its wood, some believing it to be made of walnut, while others think it may be of Java mahogany, since the *Domine* was in the Far East at one time.

(*Albany Institute of History and Art*)

§100. If family tradition be true, this safe was brought to New Netherland by Peter Lott, who arrived with his wife Geertruyd in 1652 and settled in Midwout (Flatbush), where he owned a farm on the west side of its road, a short distance south of *Het Dorp*. He helped organize the Midwout church in 1654; the certificate of his and his wife's membership is still treasured by a descendant. The safe is made of iron and is, approximately, 30 inches long and 20 inches wide and deep. It is still privately owned.

§101. Brinckerhoff family tradition claims that this desk was brought to New Netherland by Joris Dircksen and Susannah (Dubels) Brinckerhoff, who arrived in New Amsterdam in 1638. They settled on a farm in Brooklyn, where Joris was *schepen* from 1654 until 1660, and where he helped to organize its church in 1654. The desk was owned by their descendant, Emily Brinckerhoff Clapp (Mrs. Ernest), until it was acquired by the Museum in the 1930's. It is made of cedar inlaid with flowers and scrolls of beech and fruit woods. From all appearances, it might have been made in New York between 1690 and 1700.

(Museum of the City of New York)

CHAPTER SIX
Household Chattels & Personal Belongings

Plates 102-137

§102. The Cortelyou Porringer (*see caption to* §103)

Household Chattels & Personal Belongings

THE AMSTERDAM Directors of the Company were astute business men and planned to make as much money as possible out of their huge undertaking. They inserted a clause in their *Provisional Regulations for the Colonists* which stated that for the first two years after their arrival, the settlers would be provided with necessary supplies and clothing from the Company's stores "at reasonable rates," for which they could pay on the installment plan. Another clause forbade them to engage in, or to teach others, any handicraft involving commerce without special consent of the Company or its agents.

How well this second command was obeyed cannot be ascertained. For despite the fact that a great many must have lived in New Netherland, there are no braziers, coppersmiths, silversmiths, or pewterers mentioned in New Netherland records, and no spinning wheels, looms, or potters wheels listed in inventories. However, there is a ribbon-weaver named as living in Nieu Utrecht in the 1650's, one Albert Albertse Terhune. Johannes Hulster is in the Rensselaerswyck records as having been "an extraordinary potter" whose widow in 1657 sold his brick kiln to Adriaen Jansen van Ilpendam for 11,000 guilders, and his tile kiln to Pieter Meese Vroom for 3,717 guilders. But Hulster had lived in Van Rensselaer's patroonship over which the Company had no jurisdiction.

The average New Netherland household could have had all that was necessary for decent and comfortable living while the wealthier families could have enjoyed every then-known luxury. The Company's vessels arrived at New Amsterdam laden with goods of Holland manufacture. They also brought carpets from Turkey, textiles from the East Indies, African ivories, and Oriental ceramics which the Dutch East India ships had carried to Amsterdam.

An inventory of the possessions of Pieter Jacobse Marius, a merchant living in New Amsterdam as early as 1656 who died at the turn of the century, included, aside from furniture, "an old-fashioned clock, brass warming pan, stool cushions, bedstead, bed and bedding, blue curtains for window, money scales and weights, large Dutch Bible with silver tips and a silver chain and two pairs of bellows." He also owned pillow-cases, linen and muslin sheets, linen and diaper table cloths, and napkins, small linen cupboard cloths, a silver tankard, silver salt cellars, beakers, mustard pot and spoon, sweetmeat spoons, tumblers, cups with two ears, an old-fashioned salver, a mug with cover, and a baby's chafing dish as well as gold chains, rings, buckles, buttons, "ear-wire," pairs of pendants, gold and diamond rings, amber necklaces, and silver-handled knives and scissors.

§103. The Cortelyou Porringer, as this is called, has a troy weight of 4 ounces 9 grains, a circumference of 13 inches, and a depth of 1 9/16 inches. The mark on its base is attributed by Helen Burr Smith to Juriaen Blanck, Jr., who was working in New York from 1666 to 1690. The late John Marshall Philipps of Yale called this a wine taster, but it was used as a porringer by the Cortelyou family of Brooklyn. The initials, I A C, on its side indicate that it belonged to Jacques Cortelyou (born in 1662) of Nieu Utrecht, son of Jacques Cortelyou, Surveyor-General of New Netherland, and his wife, Altje I. Boerman. Their great-grandson went to live with a distant relative, Peter Cortelyou of Gowanus, Long Island, and may have taken the vessel with him. Peter, a widower in 1803, married Mary, daughter of the New York silversmith Jeronimus Alstyne who made the young couple a three-piece coffee set. He may at the same time have strengthened the delicate shell handle of the porringer by adding a silver ring, which is obviously an addition. Peter's great-grandson, Dr. Jacques Cortelyou Rushmore of Brooklyn, inherited it before he died in 1949.

§104. Peter Van Dyke, its maker, may have given this silver porringer, 5 1/8 inches in diameter, as a wedding gift to John and Maria (Cuyler) Cruger, whose initials, I C M, are on its side. The Crugers were married on December 5, 1703, the year in which Van Dyke, a relative of Maria, started working as a silversmith in New York. Cruger was Mayor of the City from 1739 until his death in 1744.
(John Devereaux Kernan)

§105. This silver porringer, made by Jacob Boelen (1657-1729) of New York, was given as a baptismal gift to Maria Van Cortlandt on September 4, 1703.
(Museum of the City of New York)

§106. This silver bowl was made by Jacob Boelen, who was working as a silversmith in New York as early as 1680. It is engraved on one side with G D H, the initials of Geertje De Hart, nee Geertje Cornelissen. She married Simon Aesen Ter Heart (De Hart) in 1664 and thereafter made her home in Gowanus, Long Island. She died sometime prior to June 19, 1691, when her husband married his second wife.

§107 & 108. Mr. John Devereaux Kernan believes that this porringer was made by Kiliaen Van Rensselaer III (1663-1719), whose mother wrote she "had him put up the shop (silversmith's) in the country" (outside Albany). The porringer belonged to Samuel and Margaret (Van Cortlandt) Bayard, married 1696, and has on its side the Bayard crest, a demi-horse within a wreath of feathery leaves. A touchmark of a demi-horse, but in reverse, is on the side of its handle. The porringer was inherited by the Bayards' daughter Margaret, who married James Van Horne in 1742. The conjoined VH on the handle is theirs.

(John Devereaux Kernan)

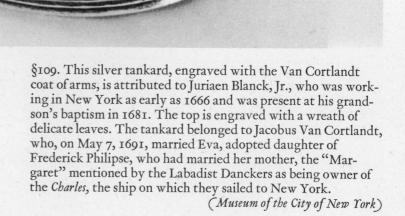

§109. This silver tankard, engraved with the Van Cortlandt coat of arms, is attributed to Juriaen Blanck, Jr., who was working in New York as early as 1666 and was present at his grandson's baptism in 1681. The top is engraved with a wreath of delicate leaves. The tankard belonged to Jacobus Van Cortlandt, who, on May 7, 1691, married Eva, adopted daughter of Frederick Philipse, who had married her mother, the "Margaret" mentioned by the Labadist Danckers as being owner of the *Charles*, the ship on which they sailed to New York.

(Museum of the City of New York)

§110. This tankard, given to the Brooklyn Museum by the Reverend
Alfred Duane Pell, was made by Romanus Moller (1661-1686), an Oslo,
Norway, silversmith. It has a six-line inscription on its side in Dutch men-
tioning Hans Rossing Kirstine Bang and the date, 1683. The top of its lid is
engraved with an elaborate, scroll-like floral motif. It is very like the silver
mug once owned by Johan Printz, Governor of New Sweden, 1642-1652, and
from which David Pietersz. de Vries wrote in his *Korte Historiael* that he had
drunk "hop beer" when he visited the Governor in 1643.

(*Brooklyn Museum*)

§111. This silver vessel with M D engraved on its side is only 1 1/4 inches high, and its diameter is but 2 5/16 inches. Made in New York in the 17th century by an unidentified silversmith, it has a conjoined VH or HA on the bottom. It could be a cup, a tumbler, or a wine taster.

The three other known pieces bearing the same mark are two silver beakers which belong to the Collegiate Reformed Protestant Dutch Church of the City of New York and a beaker in the John Marshall Phillips Collection at Yale. (*John Devereaux Kernan*)

§112. Family tradition claims that this pewter tankard was brought to New Netherland in 1656 by Pieter Cornelis Luyster, a carpenter, who settled in Nieu Amersfoort (Flatlands), married Jannetje Snediker, and later moved to Newtown, Long Island. His grandson, Johannes, born in 1691 and married to Lucretia Brower, moved to Monmouth County, New Jersey, in 1719, taking the tankard with him. He established his farm on Holland Road near Middletown and built a house in which the tankard was a treasured possession.

§113. This pewter charger is believed to have been brought to New Netherland by David Des Marest (Demarest) when he arrived on the *Bonte Koe* (Spotted Cow) in April, 1663. It was used in the house he built on the east bank of the Hackensack River, and is now owned by the family of the Reverend William Demarest of Rutgers Theological Seminary. It is pictured here through the kindness of the late Hiram Blauvelt of Oradel, New Jersey.

§114. Mrs. Arthur J. Williamson of Brooklyn owns this brass candlestick, which family tradition claims belonged to Willem Beekman, born in 1623 in Zutphen, Gelderland. He arrived at New Amsterdam on the *Princess* with the Stuyvesants, a clerk in the Company's employ. Being "an honest and polite man with ability, piety and experience," he became one of the outstanding citizens of New Netherland and later of the City of New York.

§115. For lighting their houses after dark, New Netherlanders used chandeliers of brass or copper, the *izer knaap* (iron candlestand), brass or silver candlesticks, and wooden stands for holding rushes.

This brass candlestick, made in Holland, is similar to one brought to New Netherland in 1656 by Pieter Cornelis Luyster and taken by his grandson Johannes when he moved to New Jersey. It has the circular apron for catching dripping wax which is characteristic of 17th-century Dutch candlesticks.

(Museum of the City of New York)

§116. This brass milking can, bound with copper, its strainer, and tray were made in Holland in the 17th century and were lent by their owner, Mrs. Hiram Blauvelt of Oradel, New Jersey, to the Exhibition of Dutch Colonial Heirlooms. The can is almost identical with that shown by the artist Cuyp in one of his paintings of cows.

§117. This brass horn was used for calling the farmers in from the fields at Wolvern Hoek, the property opposite Albany, New York, on which Captain Volkert Jansz. Douw settled in 1666. It is said that *Domine* Martinus Schoonmaker, "the pastor of Flatbush," had a silver horn which he used for the same purpose. Thrifty farmers, however, used a conch shell, cutting off the end of the apex and blowing through the resulting hole. It made a raucous sound that could be heard in the farthest field.

§118. This gold clasp was worn around its owner's neck by means of a ribbon attached to its gold eyes. The work of an unidentified maker, it is crudely engraved with an eagle on his perch in front of mountain peaks, all enclosed by a border of stylized tulips.

On the reverse side is the maker's mark and the letters C R, the initials of Catalyntje Rapalje, whose son, Daniel Rapalje, inherited the clasp. From him it went through seven generations of Rapaljes to Annie Maria, wife of Charles Underhill of Fishkill, New York, who was its owner in 1940.

§119 & 120. This 17th-century marriage medal is in the lid of a tankard which Tunis Johnson gave to the Brooklyn Museum in 1926. The medal was given to his ancestor, Sarah Rapalje in 1639, the year of her marriage to Hans Hansen, who arrived from Bergen, Norway, six years earlier. Around its edge is engraved, in Dutch, "See here, Lady, whom I love, here is my faith, my heart and my desire next to God alone."

The reverse of Sarah's medal reads, "Behold the Creator of Flesh and Blood created two out of one." The medal went to Sarah's daughter

Breckje Bergen, wife of Aert Middagh, who left it to their daughter Ann,
wife of Abraham Remsen. The Remsens' son Jeromus, a wealthy farmer of
Newtown, Long Island, inherited the medal, and it was he, probably, who
had the New York silversmith, Nicholas Roosevelt (made Freeman in
1735) make the tankard and set the medal in its lid. The letters J R J, for
Jeromus and Jane Remsen, are engraved on its handle. Their daughter Ann
married Barent Johnson, great-great-grandfather of the donor to the museum.   (*Brooklyn Museum*)

§121. This small silver spoon, with the mark of the silversmith Jacob Boelen (1657-1729) and the letters S D R on the underside of its bowl, was given to Sarah Danielse Rapalje when she was baptized in July, 1687. Family tradition claims the spoon to have been a name gift from her aunt, the first Sarah Rapalje, who died later that year. Sarah Danielse was the daughter of Daniel and Anna (Klock) Rapalje. She married Peter Luyster of Newtown, Long Island.

§122. It was a custom with the Dutch colonists to give memorials to mourners at a funeral, sometimes a pair of black kid gloves or a yard of white linen for a scarf. This silver spoon, made by the New York silversmith Cornelius Vander Burgh (1652-1699), was probably given at the funeral of Oloff Stevense Van Cortlandt; "O S V Cortld Obt. 1684 Apr. 4" is engraved on its bowl.

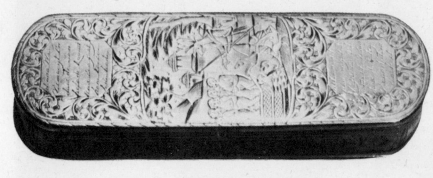

§123. These 17th-century boxes, made in Holland of brass, or of brass and copper, belong to the Albany Institute of History and Art. They were used by the Albany settlers, usually for carrying tobacco. It has been claimed that they were also used as tinder boxes.

(Albany Institute of History and Art)

§124. This silver beaker, made by an unidentified, probably Danish, silversmith about 1680, bears the name "Salt Company Participants." It was given to Andreas Dreier, a Dutchman, who had settled in Copenhagen before 1660 but who returned to Holland to sail on a Dutch man-of-war. He was with the conquering Dutch fleet in 1673 when it captured Albany and was put in command of the fort there. He was married to Gerritie Goosen Van Schaik by *Domine* Schaats of Albany. He was *schout* of the city when, after the second surrender of New Nether-land, he returned to Holland. There his six children were born. In 1699, thirteen years after his death, his widow returned to New York with two of their sons and their three daughters. (Their eldest son was an officer in the Dutch navy.) She joined the church at Coneymans, to which she left this beaker in her will.

(Albany Institute of History and Art)

§125. This large clay jug was for holding water that was brought into the house from a well. It is believed to have belonged originally to Peter Lott, who settled in Midwout (Flatbush), Long Island, in 1652. Supposedly it was made at the *steenbakkerje* (brick kiln) that was in the northeast corner of Leffert Pieterse's farm in the *Steenraap*, or northern limits, of Midwout. So much clay was extracted from the ground that a large depression formed which filled with water and became a pond on which the Flatbush youth skated until well into the 1870's.

§126. This Canton dish was used in the Freeman-Clarkson-Bergen House (1736-*ca.* 1902), which stood on Flatbush Road south of the church (northwest corner of Flatbush Avenue and Albemarle Road, Brooklyn), probably by the Cornelius Bergen family. Its design, which is under glaze in blues against a grayish-white background, is known as "Lange Eliza" and illustrates a Chinese story.

This kind of ware was made by the Chinese in the 17th, 18th, and early 19th centuries for the Western trade. It was called "India Ware" because, originally, it was carried in the East India Company's ships.

(Courtesy of Mrs. A. Lloyd Lott)

§127. This plate, decorated in blue under a white glaze, was made in China during the K'ang-hsi period (1662-1722). It was once the property of Jacob Leisler, who lived in New York on what is now the west side of Whitehall Street between Pearl and State Streets. Son of a Frankfurt clergyman, Leisler entered the service of the Company as a soldier and reached New Amsterdam in 1660. Three years later he married a rich widow, Elsie Tymense, who was a stepdaughter of Govert Loockermans, a wealthy merchant. Leisler turned merchant and made a fortune.

On Governor Dongan's fleeing from New York during the English Revolution of 1688, Leisler was chosen by the Committee of Safety to rule the Province until a new governor should arrive. Later, he was accused of treason "against Their Majesties" (William and Mary) and condemned to die. In May, 1691, he was hanged in the Market Square in front of his home and buried in his own garden. When the British Parliament reversed the decision of attainder in 1695, his body was exhumed and buried with honors in the cemetery of the Dutch Church, then in Garden Street.

(Museum of the City of New York)

§128. This dish, sometimes called a Rosewater Dish, was made in Holland between 1660 and 1700. It is 13 inches in diameter and of white earthenware decorated with small blue flowers and green leaves under a thin enamel. At the time of the American Revolution it belonged to Jacobus Lefferts, who lived on the northwest corner of the Flatbush and New Utrecht Roads, now Flatbush and Church Avenues, Brooklyn. The dish went to Lefferts's daughter Abigail, wife of Bateman Lloyd, and to their great-granddaughter, Miss Louise Garvan Zabriskie, who gave it to the Brooklyn Museum. *(Brooklyn Museum)*

§129. This plate was made in Holland and bears the mark of the Sign of the Chair. It has a diameter of 12 1/8 inches and is decorated in blue and white under a white glaze. In 1662 it belonged to Cornelis van der Hoes, who may have been a member of the Goes family which settled in Beverwyck as early as 1661. Hoes is the American corruption of that Dutch family name.

(Brooklyn Museum)

§130 & 131. These two lanterns were owned by settlers of Albany and Rensselaerswyck. The one on the left, made about 1675, is of brass with a pane of glass in its door. It has a movable, embossed piece of brass behind its candle holder and an adjustable handle by which it can be fastened to its carrier's belt. The other is of brass with a bull's-eye in its door and a movable handle at the back.

(Albany Institute of History and Art)

§132. This small box with the carved wooden lid is in the Long Island Historical Society's collection of antiques. It is said to have belonged to Gerrit Cornelisse Van Duyn, who either made it in New Netherland or brought it with him when he arrived in 1649, or on his second arrival thirty years later. A carpenter and wheelwright from Newkirk in Zeeland, he married Jacomina Jacobse Swarts in New Amsterdam in 1663. While a resident of Brooklyn in 1658, he was sued for refusing to pay toward the *domine*'s salary. Sometime after the surrender, he took his growing family to live in Zwolle, Overyssel, but, not prospering there, he returned to New York and settled on land in Nieu Utrecht, Long Island, given him by Jacques Cortelyou, the husband of his sister Neeltje.

He made his second voyage on the *Charles*, where he met the Labadists. Danckers mentions him in his Journal.

(Long Island Historical Society)

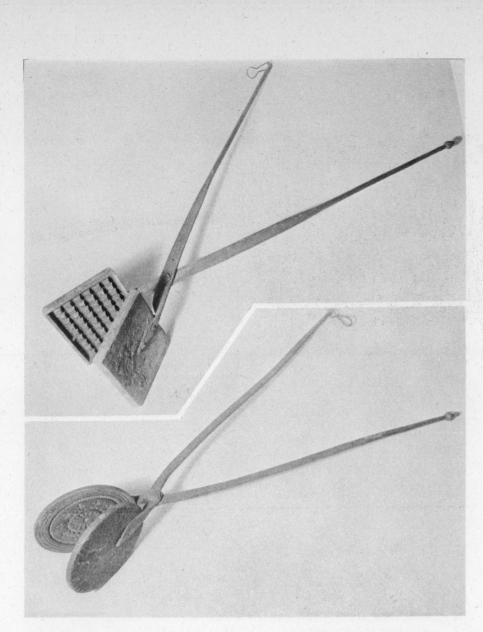

§133. These waffle irons are believed to have been made in New Jersey in the late 17th century. Today they belong to Mrs. Elmer Blauvelt of Oradel. The long handles were necessary for use on an open fire.

Waffles were such a popular food in 17th-century Netherlands that Jacob Steen even shows a waffle party in one of his genre paintings; the Pilgrim mothers learned to make waffles during their sojourn in Leiden. New Netherlanders served them frequently, and always on *Tweede Pinksterdag* (Second Whitsunday), Monday after Whitsunday, a day devoted to visiting friends and relatives.

§134. An *yzer koeckje* was a small, crisp cake baked in wafer irons. This utensil consisted of two round iron disks having long handles which could be fastened together. The disks were decorated with geometric designs that left their mark on the baked cake; sometimes with initials and a date. In New Netherland, wafer irons were given to young women for a wedding or engagement present.

§135. The shoehorn pictured, owned by John P. Luyster of Middletown, New Jersey, in 1940, is made of a cow's horn, about 15 inches long and split lengthwise. It is thought to have been brought to New Amsterdam in 1656 by Pieter Cornelisse Luyster, a carpenter, who may have carved the horn on his long voyage to New Netherland.

§136. This is the kind of oven that was used in the 17th century in The Netherlands and by the settlers of New Netherland; however, this particular example was made in the early 18th century. It belongs to the Staten Island Historical Society and is on loan at the Museum of the City of New York. The dough to be baked was placed in the oven and its lid put in place. It was then set in glowing coals and covered with them until its contents were baked to the housewife's satisfaction.

(Museum of the City of New York)

§137. This sleigh in the Melville Collection, Suffolk Museum, was made about 1770. Its design suggests that it is of Hudson Valley Dutch origin. It was built to carry six passengers, but two of its three seats have been lost. Its iron work is handwrought. It may have belonged to Peter Gansevoort of the American Revolution, for it has P. G. on its backboard. He, too, was of the Hudson Valley.

(Carriage House, Suffolk Museum, Stony Brook, Long Island)

Bibliography

ABBOTT, Wilbur C. *Colonel John Scott of Long Island* (New Haven, 1917)

ANDREWS, William Loring. *Jacob Steendam, nock vaster* (New York, 1909)

—*New Amsterdam, New Orange, and New York* (New York, 1897)

ARMBRUSTER, Eugene I. *The Eastern District of New York* (New York, 1912)

BAIRD, Henry M. *The Huguenots and Henry of Navarre* (New York, 1903)

BERGEN, Teunis G., (Transl.) Manuscript Collections of the Long Island Historical Society

—*Register of Early Settlers of Long Island* (New York, 1881)

BRODHEAD, John Romeyne. *History of the State of New York* (New York, 1863)

CORWIN, E. T. *Ecclesiastical Records of the State of New York* (Albany, 1916)

DANCKERS, Jasper. *Journal of a Voyage to New York, 1679-80* (Brooklyn, 1867) Translated by Henry C. Murphy

DE FOREST, Robert. *Jesse de Forest, Leader of Walloon Migration to America* (New York, 1923)

DEMAREST, David, D.D. *History and Characteristics of the Reformed Protestant Dutch Church* (New York, 1866)

DILLIARD, Maud Esther. *Old Dutch Houses of Brooklyn* (New York, 1945)

DITMAS, Charles A. *Historic Homesteads of Kings County* (Brooklyn, 1909)

FERNOW, Berthold. *Documents Relating to the Colonial History of the State of New York*, Vols. 12-15 (Albany, 1856-87)

—*Minutes of the Orphan Masters of New Amsterdam* (New York, 1902)

—*Records of New Amsterdam, 1653-1674* (Albany, 1897)

FISHER, Sidney George. *The Making of Pennsylvania* (Philadelphia, 1876)

Flatbush Trust Co. *Flatbush Past and Present* (Brooklyn, 1901)

GORDON, Thomas H. *History of New Jersey* (Trenton, 1834)

—*History of Pennsylvania* (Philadelphia, 1829)

HAKLUYT, Richard. *Collections of Early Voyages, Travels and Discoveries by the English Nation* (London, 1809-12)

HAZARD, Ebenezer. *Historical Collections Consisting of State Papers* (Philadelphia, 1792)

Huntington Library. *Documents Relating to New Netherland* (San Marino, 1924)

INNES, J. H. *New Amsterdam and Its People* (New York, 1892)

JAMESON, J. Franklin. *Narratives of New Netherland* (New York, 1909)

JENKINS, Stephen. *The Story of the Bronx* (New York, 1912)

KNICKERBOCKER, Diedrich (Washington Irving). *History of New York* (New York, 1826)

KNIGHT, Sarah. *Journal of a Trip to New York in* 1704 (New York, 1825)

MUNSELL, Joel. *Collections of the History of Albany* (Albany, 1865-71)

MURPHY, Henry C. *Anthology of New Netherland* (New York, 1865)

O'CALLAGHAN, E. B. *Calendar of New York Historical Manuscripts* (Albany, 1865)
   —*Documentary History of the State of New York* (Albany, 1860)
   —*Documents Relating to the Colonial History of the State of New York*, Vols. I-II (Albany, 1856-87)
   —*History of New Netherland* (New York, 1846-48)
   —*Laws and Ordinances of New Netherland* (Albany, 1866)

ONDERDONCK, Henry. *History of Friends on Long Island* (Jamaica, L. I., 1851)
   —*Long Island in the Olden Times* (Jamaica, L. I., 1851)

PRIME, Nathaniel S. *History of Long Island* (New York, 1845)

PURCHAS, Samuel. *Purchas, His Pilgrimage*, 3rd Ed. (London, 1817)

Records of the Town of North and South Hempstead, Long Island (Jamaica, L. I., 1896)

REYNOLDS, Cuyler. *Albany Chronicles* (Albany, 1906)

RIKER, James. *History of Harlem* (Elizabeth, N. J., 1904)

RIKER, James, Jr. *The Annals of Newtown in Queens County* (New York, 1852)

SANFORD, Elias B. *History of Connecticut* (Hartford, 1890)

SCHARF, J. Thomas. *History of Westchester County, N. Y.* (Philadelphia, 1886)

SCHENCK, P. L., M.D. *Historical Sketch of the Zabriskie Homestead* (Brooklyn, 1881)

SINGLETON, Esther. *Dutch New York* (New York, 1909)

STILES, Henry R. *History of Kings County* (New York, 1884)
   —*History of the City of Brooklyn, A* (Brooklyn, 1867)

STILLWELL, William H. *History of the Reformed Protestant Dutch Church of Gravesend* (Gravesend, L. I., 1872)

STOKES, I. N. Phelps. *Iconography of Manhattan Island* (New York, 1918)

STONE, William L. *History of the City of New York* (New York, 1872)

STRONG, Thomas M. *The History of the Town of Flatbush* (New York, 1842)

THOMPSON, Benjamin F. *History of Long Island* (New York, 1839)

Two hundred fiftieth Anniversary of the Settlement of the Jews in the United States (New York, 1906)

VALENTINE, David T. *History of the City of New York* (New York, 1853)
  —*Manuals of the Corporation of the City of New York* (New York, 1841-70)
VANDERBILT, Gertrude Lefferts. *The Social History of Flatbush* (New York, 1881)
VAN LAER, A. J. F., Ed. *Correspondence of Jeremias Van Rensselaer* (Albany, 1932)
  —*Court Minuits of Fort Orange and Beverwyck* (Albany, 1920-23)
  —*Van Rensselaer Bowier Manuscripts* (New York, 1906)
VAN RENSSELAER, Mrs. John King. *The Goede Vrouw of Mana-ha-ta* (New York, 1912)
VAN VALEN, J. M. *History of Bergen County, N. J.* (New York, 1900)
VAN WINKLE, Edward. *Manhattan, 1624-1639* (New York, 1916)
VAN WYCK, Frederick. *Keskachauge, First White Settlement on Long Island* (New York, 1924)
VERSTEEG, Dingman. *Sketch of the Early History of the Reformed Dutch Church of Bergen in Jersey City* (New York, 1889)
WELLS, Cornelius L., D. D. *Quarter Millenium Anniversary of the Reformed Dutch Church of Flatbush, New York* (Brooklyn, 1904)
WILSON, James Grant. *Memorial History of the City of New York* (New York, 1892)
WOOD, Silas. *Sketch of the First Settlement of Several Towns on Long Island* (Brooklyn, 1828)

ADDITIONAL SOURCES

Collections of the Holland Society of New York
Collections of the New York Genealogical and Biographical Society
Collections of the New-York Historical Society
Genealogies of many of the families descended from the New Netherland settlers

Maps

THE COMMUNITIES IN NEW NETHERLAND

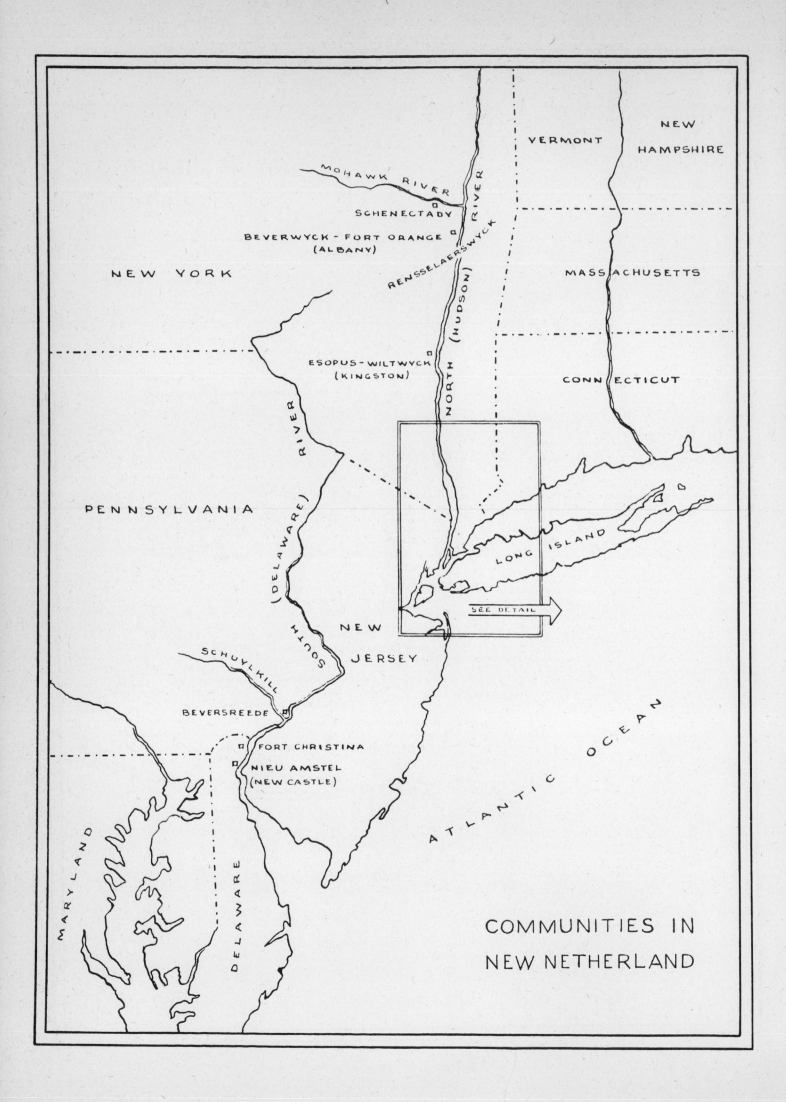

COMMUNITIES IN
NEW NETHERLAND

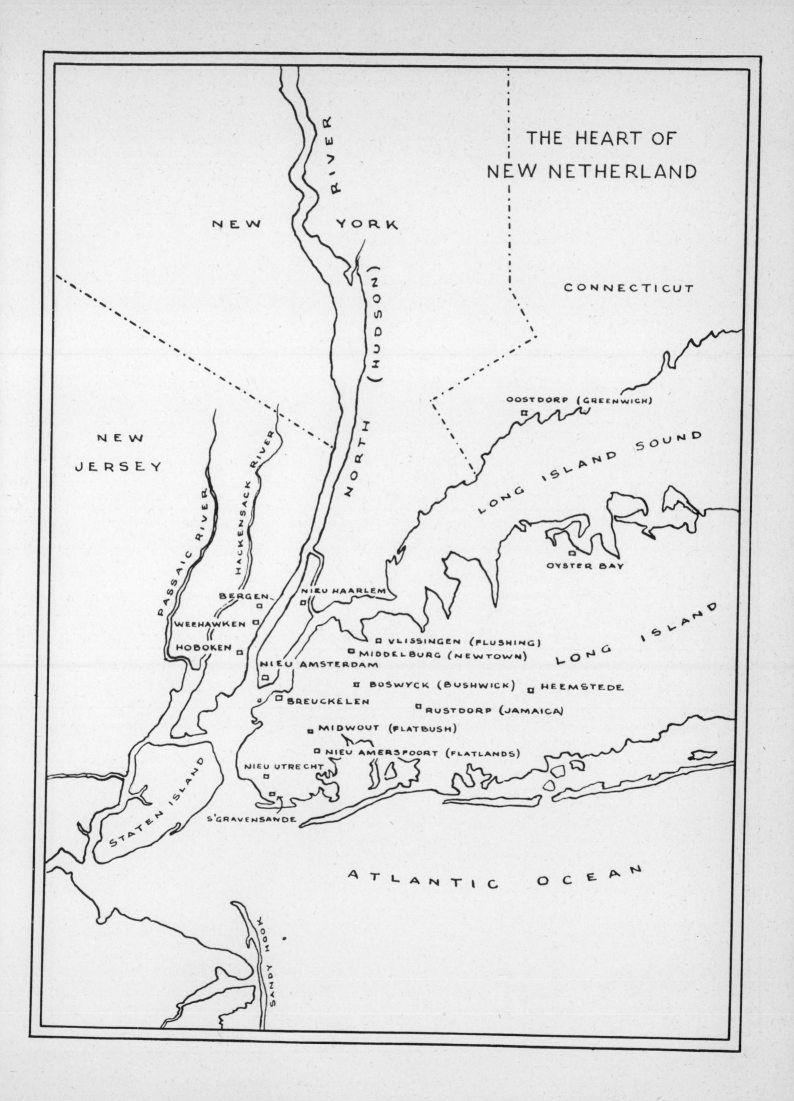

THE HEART OF
NEW NETHERLAND

NEW YORK

NEW JERSEY

CONNECTICUT

RIVER

NORTH (HUDSON) RIVER

PASSAIC RIVER

HACKENSACK RIVER

OOSTDORP (GREENWICH)

LONG ISLAND SOUND

OYSTER BAY

LONG ISLAND

BERGEN

NIEU HAARLEM

WEEHAWKEN

HOBOKEN

NIEU AMSTERDAM

BREUCKELEN

VLISSINGEN (FLUSHING)

MIDDELBURG (NEWTOWN)

BOSWYCK (BUSHWICK)

HEEMSTEDE

RUSTDORP (JAMAICA)

MIDWOUT (FLATBUSH)

NIEU AMERSFOORT (FLATLANDS)

NIEU UTRECHT

STATEN ISLAND

S'GRAVENSANDE

ATLANTIC OCEAN

SANDY HOOK

Typographical design & layout by
Peter Brogren
for Book Craft Inc., Tokyo
The text was set in
'Monotype' Van Dijck

Typographical design & layout by
Peter Brogren
for Book Craft Inc., Tokyo
The text was set in
'Monotype' Van Dijck